PETRONIUS:
CENA TRIMALCHIONIS

PETRONIUS: CENA TRIMALCHIONIS

Edited with Notes by the late

Thomas Cutt <small>WAYNE STATE UNIVERSITY</small>

Introduction to the Revised Edition by

Jacob E. Nyenhuis <small>WAYNE STATE UNIVERSITY</small>

WAYNE STATE UNIVERSITY PRESS, DETROIT 1970

Published simultaneously in Canada
by The Copp Clark Publishing Company
517 Wellington Street, West
Toronto 2B, Canada.

Library of Congress Catalog Card Number 73-105090
Standard Book Number 8143-1410-4

WAYNE STATE UNIVERSITY CLASSICAL TEXTS SERIES

Jacob E. Nyenhuis, *General Editor*

PETRONIUS: *CENA TRIMALCHIONIS*

PLAUTUS: *AMPHITRUO*

CONTENTS

PREFACE

This edition of Petronius' *Cena Trimalchionis* by the late Professor Thomas Cutt has been used in experimental form at Wayne State University since 1961. Its success has encouraged us to issue an edited text of Petronius' *Cena* as the first volume in the Wayne State University Press Classical Texts Series. In response to the suggestions offered by my colleagues who have used the text a lengthier introduction has been added to increase the usefulness of this edition. Since Professor Cutt's first concern was always his students, the text is naturally oriented toward their needs, but sound scholarship underlies every aspect of it; I have tried to emulate him in the writing of this introduction. If this act of *pietas* performed in memory of a highly respected and deeply loved colleague meets with the approval of both students and scholars, my efforts will have achieved the fullest possible reward.

Acknowledgement of gratitude is due not only to Mrs. Thomas Cutt, who graciously consented to the publication of this copyrighted material under my editorship, but also to my colleagues in the Greek and Latin Department at Wayne State University who offered valuable suggestions: Mrs. Norma

Goldman and Professors Ernest J. Ament, John L. Lazzatti, Jr., and Richard W. Minadeo. Appreciation is also due the students who participated in the experimentation with this text and to the director of Wayne State University Press, Dr. Harold A. Basilius, for his vision and courage in embarking upon this new series.

Jacob E. Nyenhuis
April, 1970

INTRODUCTION TO THE REVISED EDITION

THE AUTHOR: PETRONIUS

The inquisitive reader asks, Who was Petronius? but he finds no sure answer to his questions, for scholars have disputed not only the period in which Petronius lived and wrote but even his very name. To the extent that agreement is possible, however, it is now generally agreed that the author of the *Satyricon* and the Petronius described by Tacitus *(Annals* 16.18-19) must be identical. This conclusion is based on the hypothesis that only an individual like Tacitus' Petronius could have written the spicy *Satyricon;* serious 19th century scholars also argued that the diction, the content, the characters and the historical conditions were appropriate only to the time of Nero, the middle of the 1st century A.D. Circumstantial evidence thus convicts Tacitus' Petronius of the "crime" of writing the *Satyricon.* The vivid description of this extraordinary individual is worth reading on its own merits, but it deserves inclusion here because acquaintance with the character of the man who presumably wrote the lively satirical novel, the *Satyricon,* will undoubtedly increase our enjoyment as we read the *Cena Trimalchionis (Trimalchio's Dinner)* which is an ex-

cerpt from the novel. The following three paragraphs are translated directly from a passage in the *Annals* (16.17-19) of
Tacitus, in which he is describing events of the year 66 A.D.:

Within a few days in the same troop fell Annaeus
Mela, Cerialis Anicius, Rufrius Crispinus and Gaius
Petronius . . . .

Petronius deserves brief mention beyond the others.
His days were spent in sleep, his nights in the duties
and amusements of life. Whereas other men won their
reputation by hard work, he won his through idleness.
Yet he was not regarded as a debauchee and spendthrift,
like most of those who are prodigal of self and sub-
stance, but he was a man of exquisite art in his extravagance. The more his words and actions proved unconven-
tional and displayed an air of carelessness, the more they
were accepted because of their apparent freshness.
Nevertheless, as proconsul of Bithynia and later as consul, he proved himself vigorous and skillful in his tasks.
Then, because he reverted to his life of vice or else because of his pretence of such a life, he was accepted
among Nero's few most intimate associates as his referee
on taste *(elegantiae arbiter)* so long as Nero in his
sensual affluence thought nothing charming or luxurious
except what Petronius had approved. On this account the
jealousy of Tigellinus was aroused against an apparent
rival who seemed his superior in the art of self indulgence; he therefore appealed to the emperor's dominant
passion, his cruelty, by accusing Petronius of friend-
ship with Scaevinus,[1] after bribing one of Petronius'
slaves to turn informer and imprisoning the majority of
the remaining slaves. No opportunity for defence was
offered.

It happened that the emperor was in Campania at that
time; when Petronius (enroute to join the emperor) had
traveled as far as Cumae, he was arrested and held in
custody there. He neither put up with the delays offered
by hope and fear, nor did he end his life with precipitous
haste, but he severed his veins, then bound them up,
then reopened them, to suit his fancy, and conversed with
friends, not seriously nor with a display of bravado to

---

[1]Scaevinus was a senator who had joined Gaius Piso and others
(including the poet Lucan) in a major conspiracy against the
emperor during the previous year.

gain a reputation for his steadiness. He also listened to them while they recited, not discourses on the immortality of the soul and the consolations of philosophy, but lively songs and lighthearted verse. He dealt out rewards to some of his slaves, beatings to others. He dined, then napped, that his death, however compulsory, might appear to be due to natural causes. Not even in his will did he, like so many people on their deathbeds, flatter Nero or Tigellinus or any other person of rank, but instead he listed the scandalous acts and the originality of each sexual union of the emperor, together with the names of his out-worn sexual mates, male and female alike. He sealed it and sent it to Nero; then he broke his signet ring to avoid its subsequent misuse to endanger others.[2]

William Arrowsmith, in the introduction (p. vii) to his translation of the *Satyricon,* sums up the description of this Petronius and the arguments for identifying him as the author of the *Satyricon:* "Unconventionality, charm, courage, refinement, an appetite for pleasure, a dislike of heroic postures and an understanding of others: if we had to imagine for ourselves the probable character of the Petronius who wrote the *Satyricon,* it is exactly these qualities we should be compelled to select. Which is to say that a sound principle of economy supports the claim of Tacitus' Petronius to be the author of the *Satyricon.* Such a man would have been a rarity in any age, and those who reject Gaius Petronius' authorship of the *Satyricon* must accept the responsibility for finding a more likely candidate."

THE WORK: THE *SATYRICON*

The *Satyricon* has not been preserved in its entirety for us. In fact, if there is any truth in the statement contained in a manuscript discovered during the 17th century, only a very

---

[2]After Lucan's execution for his complicity in a conspiracy against Nero (Tacitus *Annals* 15.49ff. and 15.70), his father, Annaeus Mela, was also implicated in the plot by means of a forged letter (Tacitus *Annals* 16.17), presumably sealed with Lucan's signet ring.

small portion of the novel has survived the ravages of time and the accidents of fate, for the manuscript states that its excerpts (which comprise a major portion of the extant *Satyricon*) are "fragments from the fifteenth and sixteenth books."[3]

It is impossible to reconstruct with any certainty the complete story of the novel or even to determine its true length, but the surviving excerpts are sufficiently lengthy and coherent to enable us to offer more than a bare outline of the plot. On the surface, the central theme appears merely to be the escapades of two friends, Encolpius and Ascyltus, told in first-person narrative by Encolpius. Although their deeds and misdeeds are recounted with great relish and at considerable length, even a superficial reading reveals a greater depth of artistic purpose, while a careful reading will uncover many additional insights and deeper levels of meaning. The forthrightness of the narrative and its content may shock the modesty of some readers, but the novel, in spite of its fragmentation, continues to attract and entertain a large circle of readers.

The gullible Encolpius (literally, "lap" or "crotch"—we might call him "Mr. Crotch") is depicted as the victim of persecution by an angered deity, Priapus, who was a predominantly phallic ancient fertility god.[4] Because of many

---

[3]The manuscript, discovered by Marino Statileo around 1650 A.D. at Trau (in Dalmatia) in the library of Nicolo Cippico, consists of 248 pages, including 11 blank pages, and is written in a 15th century hand. In addition to portions of Petronius, the manuscript contains elegies of Catullus, Propertius and Tibullus, and the imaginary letter of Sappho to Phaon from Ovid's elegiac *Heroides*. The text of Petronius contained in this manuscript consists of about 20 pages of excerpts (described as *vulgaria excerpta*, or the common excerpts) and about 24 pages containing the complete episode of Trimalchio's banquet; although derived from different sources (manuscript traditions), these two parts of the *Satyricon* were copied by the same hand (scribe).

[4]William Arrowsmith (Petronius, *The Satyricon*, Ann Arbor, 1959) offers (p. 169) the following description of Priapus: "He was originally worshiped at Lampsacus on the Hellespont, and from here his worship spread to Greece and Rome. The attribute of Priapus is the phallus, and indeed, as represented in art, he is little more than

allusions and parallels, Encolpius has been interpreted as a kind of comic Odysseus, pursued on land and sea not by an angered major god, Poseidon, but by an angry minor phallic deity. Encolpius' companion and accomplice, Ascyltus, generally succeeds in avoiding the suffering inflicted upon Encolpius; hence his name Ascyltus, which means "undisturbed," "not bothered," "not harassed." (Should we call him "Mr. Cool"?) Indeed, Ascyltus is often a source of misery for his companion, for he also plays the rival to Encolpius for the affection of his beloved youth Giton and, upon occasion, steals this treasure from the beleaguered and intensely jealous Encolpius.

Into the lives of these young men comes an immense variety of interesting types of people who, through the author's artistry, become far more than mere types. Among these fascinating characters are the bombastic and bombarded poet Eumolpus; the licentious exile and ex-lover of Encolpius, Tryphaena; the ill-fated ship-owner Lichas; the noble but degraded Circe; and Priapus' priestess, Quartilla, and her seductive attendants with their supply of aphrodisiacs. All of these add color to the narrative of the seemingly countless scrapes encountered by our narrator and his companions. None of these, however, is as well known as the *nouveau*

---

a very slightly humanized phallus. He is also, as a vegetation god, a deity of the garden, protecting and aiding the sexual processes of nature . . . he seems to have been a figure of fun, broadly but lightly, in a tolerant sense, obscene. He is . . . a minor genius of sexual potency, a domesticated but unreliable lord of lust." Dinnage, in the introduction to his translation of Petronius (pp. x-xi), further illuminates this subject with these observations: "The deformed son of Venus, Priapus was a deity presiding over gardens, more as a kind of scarecrow than a dignitary, and a deity whose diocese extended over the genitals and parts of generation of both sexes. While the *carmina priapea* [songs dedicated to Priapus—Ed.] give ample evidence of the god's liberal-minded grossness, there were doubtless matters concerning sex that especially irked him. Impotence would be one of them, homosexuality another. Their occurrence and subsequent punishment may well be the connecting link of the *Satyricon,* although the sheer continuity of intrigue and adventure is sufficient, in retrospect, to place it at the head of a whole tradition of picaresque literature."

riche freedman, Trimalchio, the central figure of the narrative contained in this volume, for the story of Trimalchio and his elaborately ostentatious festal entertainments is by itself a widely read masterpiece of literary craftsmanship.

The *Satyricon* is a work of amazing versatility, in style as well as in subject matter. It ranges from tales of all forms of lechery and perversion to satire and sophisticated irony, to denunciation of contemporary education with its emphasis on irrelevant and out-moded rhetoric, to scathing literary criticism, with parodies of poetry of Nero and Lucan, to delightful Milesian tales (including the story of a matron of Ephesus dramatized by Christopher Fry in his *A Phoenix Too Frequent),* to accounts of intrigue and roguery. Remarkable in its insight into human character, the *Satyricon* displays its author's uncanny ability to shift his style to fit his shifting characters. They come alive through their speech, with the result that a few words from the mouth of a newly introduced character create a clear and distinct picture worth a thousand words of descriptive narrative.

The novel is a wide-ranging commentary on contemporary, everyday life and practices, displaying all the pretentiousness of Neronian Rome, but it also illustrates many human foibles characteristic of people in nearly every age, thus giving it an immediacy in our time as well. One excerpt, for example, perceptively and poignantly comments on the unpredictability and mutability of fortune, while another draws a moral on the influence of money on the administration of justice. Equally commendable and noteworthy is his skillful adaptation of literary predecessors, such as Virgil, to achieve a sophisticated ironic effect. As with other classical authors, it is indeed disappointing to possess such fragmentary and tantalizing portions of what must have been a work of great genius.

THE GENRE – or, HOW DO WE CLASSIFY THE WORK?

I have already used the words "novel" and "satirical novel" to describe the *Satyricon,* but these terms represent only a very limited number of attempts at classifying this work. It has also been variously described as a romance, a picaresque romance, a prose epic, an epic of the beggar student, a kind of burlesque or mock-epic, a novel of adventure combined with a copious literary miscellany, a satire, a Menippean satire, and "a satirical comedy based upon a fictional narrative both episodic and recognizably picaresque in nature," to name just a few of the combinations suggested by scholarly critics. Part of the problem of classification is attributable to the rather fragmentary nature of the work, but it is also partly due to the great versatility and elusiveness of the work itself, since it seems to include examples and parodies of so many different genres. Before I offer my own descriptive phrase to add to the proliferation of technical terms, I should perhaps further clarify and define some of the terms already mentioned.

The term satire is undoubtedly familiar to every prospective reader of this book, both in its usage to describe poetry or prose which holds up human vices to ridicule or scorn and in its employment for the description of any trenchant wit, irony or sarcasm used to expose and discredit vice or folly. The word itself is derived from the Latin noun *satura,* originally meaning 'a dish filled with various ingredients (usually fruits), a medley,' and subsequently extended to mean 'a literary form loosely combining a variety of topics' which was employed for the censorious description of human foibles.[5] Quintilian's oft-quoted *satura quidem tota nostra est* claims satire as a unique and independent Roman invention, and Lucilius (second c. B.C.) is credited both with establishing dactylic hexameter as the appropriate metrical vehicle for satire and with the use of *satura* for the purposes of polemic and invective. Lucilius' work exists today in only fragmentary form, but the satirical poetry of Horace (65-8 B.C.), Persius (34-62 A.D.) and Juvenal (mid-first to second c. A.D.) has been well preserved. The title of Petronius' work, moreover,

---

[5]*Satura* is a feminine substantive developed from the adjective *satur, satura, saturum,* meaning 'full, sated' (cf. *satis).*

has been variously explained as derived from either *satura* or the Greek word *satyrikos,* i.e. concerned with satyrs (the riotously merry and lascivious satyrs are familiarly depicted in art as sylvan dieties in essentially human form, but with the ears and tail of a horse or goat and in a perpetual state of sexual excitement). Although the *Satyricon* is, or rather contains, satire in this tradition, the contrast between his work and the other satirists is clearly illustrated not only in his lightness of touch and in the deftness and subtlety of his humor, but especially in the range and variety of style, of content and of perspective and attitude.

Another variety of satire, called Menippean satire, was introduced into Latin literature by Varro (116-27 B.C.; he was older but virtually contempory with Caesar and Cicero, although he outlived them both). This distinctive type of satire derives its name from Menippus of Gadara (in Syria), a third-century B.C. Cynic philosopher, who mingled prose and poetry in his humorous treatment of philosophical themes, presumably parodying and burlesquing the works of the authors whom he was ridiculing, just as Aristophanes had earlier parodied Euripides in the *Frogs.* Menippus had been preceded by Timon of Phlius (ca. 315-226 B.C.) in the use of poetry as a vehicle for humorous satirical narrative aimed at philosophy and philosophers for their loss of dignity and at various other social follies, but Menippus originated the alternating of prose and poetry and further refined the art. Varro deliberately imitated the style of Menippus (as Cicero, *Academica posteriora* 2.8, indicates) in 150 books of *Satirae Menippeae;* only short fragments of this voluminous work remain to illustrate his use of this frolicsome medium to communicate his wise and serious reflections on life and people. The development of this form of satire by the Greeks would seem to contradict Quintilian's claim, but his assertion is defensible if interpreted as meaning that the Romans alone achieved complete development and mastery of the art of satire. Insofar as Petronius mingled prose and poetry, parody and serious narration, short story and epic, realism and philosophy, he was placing himself in the tradition of Menippean satire Romanized by Varro and further employed by Petronius' contemporary at Nero's court, Seneca, in his satirizing of the emperor Claudius (41-54 A.D.) in his *Apocolocyntosis* ("Pumpkinification of Claudius"). Thus, in a certain formal sense, it is quite legitimate to describe the *Satyricon* as an example of Menippean satire, but his work is far more complex and sophisticated than these earlier forms of moralizing.

Clearly, also, there are romantic elements, such as the Milesian tales, in the *Satyricon,* and surely it is picaresque in that it has a rogue as its hero.[6] In this sense it can be said to anticipate such so-called picaresque romances originating in 16th century Spain as *Lazarillo de Tormes* and *Guzman de Alfarache.*[7] There are also epic elements and there is burlesque of the epic mode in this multifaceted work, but it clearly is more than any one of these.

What, then, is the *Satyricon?* The easy (or, rather, the cowardly) answer is to declare that it contains such a variety of genres that it defies classification, that it can only be described as a potpourri of various genres. Although the coward's reply contains more than a germ of truth, I believe that a suitable descriptive term can be found. I would call it a comic-satirical novel, thus placing it in the broad genre of the novel, while also accounting for both its satirical and its lighter comic elements.

---

[6]The Spanish word for rogue is *picaro.* The picaresque novel is defined as a kind of novel of adventure which presents a "prose autobiography of a real or fictitious personage who describes his experiences as a social parasite, and who satirizes the society which he has exploited" (*Encyclopaedia Britannica* [1952 ed.] 17,905).

[7]In his *Don Quixote* and other novels Cervantes skillfully depicts the picaresque life; there also were many imitations and adaptations of the picaresque novel outside of Spain, with *Gil Blas* as one of the better-known and more successful examples.

THE EXCERPT: TRIMALCHIO'S DINNER

The *Cena Trimalchionis* represents the most complete and unified segment of the *Satyricon* that has been preserved. As such, it best illustrates the creative genius of Petronius, revealing him to us as a brilliant master of the art of satirical communication and as a skillful and facile writer equally capable of expressing light and versatile humor and capturing the subtle nuances of character portrayal through descriptive narrative and spoken word.

In the *Cena,* as in the rest of the novel, Encolpius narrates the story in the first person. His comrades throughout this segment are Ascyltus and Giton, and they are present at Trimalchio's dinner because of the ability of their acquaintance, the rhetorician Agamemnon, to wangle invitations to dinner at the homes of the class of wealthy freedmen typified by Trimalchio. At the conclusion of the banquet they succeed in eluding this boring rhetorician, but his place is soon taken by the bothersome poet Eumolpus.

Structurally the *Cena* is based on the Menippean symposium, which in turn presumably was an imitation and adaptation of Plato's *tour de force,* the *Symposium* but, aside from two very brief excursions into poetry (chapters 34 and 55), the admixture of prose and poetry characteristic of the Menippean mode is totally absent. Like Plato, however, Petronius very carefully constructs his description of the dinner party, although his purposes in composing the work obviously are far removed from the lofty Platonic ideals. Nonetheless, his character portrayal through speeches, like Plato's, is highly successful, but his technique is so thoroughly refined that even the vocabulary and syntax, as well as the content, of the speeches reveal not only the intellectual processes of the speakers but even the level of their education and their social status, while also holding up their pretensions for amusement and scorn. The description of social customs (mainly of the middle classes), although undoubtedly of great value to the antiquarian, is likely to interest and amuse even the casual modern reader, for it provides us with an insight into daily life in southern Italy during the Neronian era.[8]

In brief, the plot and setting for the *Cena* are as follows: as the scene opens, our heroes are aroused from their gloom with a reminder of their invitation to Trimalchio's lavish party; at the baths they get their first glimpse of their host and his vulgar display of wealth, then they follow him to his house, where they are astonished by its ostentatious appointments (26-30). Hors d'oeuvres for the guests precede the grand entrance of the host, who rudely continues a game of dice (31-33a). The progression of extravagant displays of the host's wealth continues with elegant and novel dishes, including the best vintage wine and one course served with food appropriate to each of the twelve signs of the zodiac (33b-36). After a brilliant aside in which Encolpius' table-mate reveals his own character while describing the hostess, the host and several other guests, Trimalchio interrupts with an amusing discourse on astrology, interpreting the signs of the zodiac (37-39). The seemingly endless procession of elaborate culinary treats is broken by the host's atrocious puns (40-41c). Trimalchio's temporary departure from the room provides an opportunity for the presentation of a series of skillful vignettes of Dama, Seleucus, Phileros, Ganymedes and Echion (41d-46). Upon his return, he discourses on constipation, orders a hog slain and roasted, prattles on in ignorant confusion about mythological stories, and perpetrates, for his amusement, an elaborate hoax upon the guests, followed by further execrable puns and garbled stories (47-52). A reading of the day's financial report further illustrates Trimalchio's vast wealth, but it is interrupted when a stunt-man topples on the host, causing universal bedlam; after recovering from the accident, he composes a poem to immortalize the occasion and quotes a poem of Publilius in support of his literary criticism of Cicero's and Publilius' poetry (53-55). A series of grotesque conundrums

---

[8]Jerome Carcopino's *Daily Life in Ancient Rome* (transl. by E. O. Lorimer, ed. by Henry T. Rowell, New Haven, 1940) draws heavily upon the *Cena* for information about bathing, banqueting and certain other social practices.

evokes uncontrollable laughter from Ascyltus and Giton, a heated rebuke from Hermeros (a fellow freedman of Trimalchio's), and a gentle rebuke to all from the host (56-59). The ceiling panels open to permit descent of a hoop filled with party favors for the guests, Niceros tells the first recorded account of a werewolf and Trimalchio parries with a yarn about witches who stole an infant from his cradle and substituted a straw doll (60-63). Trimalchio's effusions toward his pet slave and his dog are followed by yet another course of the meal forced upon the guests, but their attention is distracted by the arrival of Trimalchio's friend, Habinnas, an imperial cult official and stone mason, who is already half-drunken from a previous party, which he describes in considerable detail, at Trimalchio's urging (64-66). Habinnas demands the appearance of Trimalchio's wife, Fortunata, who enters and directly engages Habinnas' wife, Scintilla, in a vulgar contest of displaying expensive jewelry and in other idle feminine gossip interrupted by Habinnas' drunken horseplay (67). Dessert is served, accompanied by an atrocious and offensive misquoting of Virgil, a brief lovers' spat between host and hostess over a slave, and entertainment by Habinnas' slave (whose two defects were that he was circumcized and he snored); guests are anointed, slaves are admitted and there follows a maudlin scene occasioned by Trimalchio's reading of his will, his describing of the tomb he wants erected for him by Habinnas and his composing of his own epitaph, thus eliciting tears from his entire household (68-72a). The party moves into another room for a bath, then resumes its carousing in yet another dining room (72-73). A serious quarrel between Trimalchio and Fortunata erupts with the result that he utterly disowns her and creates another maudlin scene; then he sentimentally reminisces about his rise to fame and fortune, orders that his funeral finery be brought in, that a funeral march be played and that he be eulogized by the guests while he farcically lies in state; the band's trumpeting disrupts the party, for the firemen rush in, thinking that the house is on fire, and in the ensuing confusion our picaresque trio slips out of the house, eluding Agamemnon (74-78). Thus the party and this segment of the story end.

THE CAST: CHARACTERS AND CHARACTERIZATION

The host of the *Cena*, Trimalchio, is so highly visual and so interestingly and adroitly portrayed that it seems only reasonable to sketch his story and his character first.

Trimalchio's name is a Latin-Semitic hybrid meaning "thrice-blessed"; it thus reveals his origin in the Near East. Brought to Rome from Asia as a slave in his early youth, he was his master's favorite (and his mistress', too, he boasts) for 14 years, became master in the house and was made co-heir with the emperor, coming out of it with the fortune of a senator which he built into a vast fortune (chapters 75-76): an entire wall at the entrance to his home was painted with frescoes hybristically detailing, with appropriate labels, each step in his career, from his sale at the slave market to his role as apprentice accountant, next as paymaster, and, finally, to his elevation to a position as an official of the imperial cult; apparently to give it epic proportions, the frescoes of his career also contained, at the center, scenes from the *Iliad* and *Odyssey*, while in a corner at the end of the portico he displayed the clippings of his first beard in a golden pyx (chest) set prominently in a shrine decked with silver household gods and a marble Venus (chapter 29).[9] Every aspect of the description of the dinner party is designed to emphasize the vulgar display of his wealth. In his self-composed epitaph (71e), Trimalchio assesses his fortunes at 30 million sesterces: although this sum falls short of the 100 million sesterces attributed to the fortune-hunter Africanus by Martial (12.10), it vastly exceeds the 400,000 sesterces which constituted the property qualifications for a Knight *(Eques)*, an amount which Juvenal (14.322-28) proclaims as an adequate sum to provide happiness for a wise man.[10]

---

[9] On the religious rite associated with the first shaving of the beard, see Carcopino, *Daily Life in Ancient Rome*, pp. 160-61.

[10] A yearly income of 20,000 sesterces was considered a "vital minimum" to maintain a Roman citizen (Juvenal 9.140-41); this

A few examples will suffice to illustrate the vulgarity with which Trimalchio flaunts his wealth. He has a large clock in his dining room and a bugler stationed beside it to announce the passing of each hour (chapter 26); when he plays ball, he never bothers to pick one up, but has a slave with a huge sack of balls to toss out a new one whenever one is missed, not to mention the two eunuchs who stand by during the game, the one to keep score, the other to hold the silver chamber pot when his master wants to relieve himself (27). It is super-fluous to mention the innumerable culinary delicacies served up to the guests, for these illustrations of ostentation are interwoven throughout the *Cena,* but mention should be made of the wine: Trimalchio serves wine in bottles labeled "Falernian wine of the vintage of Opimius, 100 years old" and informs the guests that on the previous day he had served cheaper wine, although his guests were more important (34).[11] Later he declares that if the guests dislike the wine he will serve another variety, and adds that he fortunately does not have to pay for his wine, since it comes from a new estate of his, gratuitously adding "As yet I know nothing about it, but it is said to be close to the Tarracinians and the Tarentines. Now I would like to add Sicily to my estate that I may travel through my own land when it suits my fancy to go to Africa" (48).[12] Almost immediately he boasts of possessing two

---

amount was the annual yield of an estate of 400,000 sesterces and was barely adequate to maintain modest middle class standards in Trajan's day (98-117 A.D.), while Pliny the Younger contended that he was not rich, although his estate approaches 20 million sesterces. For further information on this, see Carcopino, pp. 65-70.

[11]For the absurdity of this, see the note on 34 c.

[12]See Cutt's note on 48a. Although he may be displaying his ig-norance of geography here, as Cutt suggests, this may merely be a megalomaniacal statement matching his expressed desire to purchase Sicily: he seems to me to suggest here that he owns all the land from Tarracina (in Latium) to Tarentum (on the coast of Magna Graecia), impossible even for a man of his wealth; his boast is comparable to this assertion which I once heard: "My father-in-law owns half of New Hampshire." Later Trimalchio asserts, "If I could merely add Apulia to my estate, I could die content" (77).

libraries, one Latin and one Greek, and when Agamemnon begins to honor his request for a report on the day's debate topic, beginning with the words "a rich man and a poor man were at odds," Trimalchio rudely and with colossal impudence interrupts with the disdainful remark "What is a poor man?" disrupting any further discussion on such a topic as poverty, either to show its unreality for him or because he does not wish to be reminded of his former position. Numerous additional examples could be cited, but one final instance will suffice: he orders Habinnas (probably for the hundredth time) to construct for him a tomb 100 feet wide and 200 feet long, surrounded by a vineyard of every variety of fruit tree known to man and ornamented with numerous statues and carvings and with a sundial in the center so that anyone seeking the time of day will have to read his name (71).

Trimalchio is a triumph of realistic portraiture on a grand scale of the type of enormously wealthy freedman forming a class of *nouveau riche* that resulted from the system which forbade Romans of noble birth to engage in trade. He thus typifies the individual in any society whose economic advancement has vastly outstripped his social and cultural development, resulting in the crude, insensitive and vulgar rich man of the type nearly as evident in America today as in the 1920's, for example, or in Rome during the early empire. His guests include other millionaire freedmen such as the wealthy undertaker, Proculus, and the stone mason, Habinnas, and a former stevedore, Diogenes, who used to tote wood on his shoulders (38 and 65ff.); the party is rounded out with parasites like Professor (of Rhetoric) Agamemnon, who are invited to give some class to the party and to inflate the ego of the host by their obsequiousness. Trimalchio's acuteness in financial affairs is hardly matched by intellectual awareness: his pretense at literary criticism is exposed when he quotes a third-rate poem (55), his absurdly inaccurate knowledge of mythological stories is demonstrated by his confusion of Cassandra for Medea, Niobe for Pasiphaë and the Trojan Horse for Pasiphaë's wooden cow (52) or Ganymede and Diomedes for Castor and Pollux, Agamemnon for Menelaus and

Helen for Iphigenia (59), to cite just a few examples. The level of his education is further illustrated by his droll comments on astrology (39) and by his superstitiousness when a cock crows (74); his philosophy is that man is inconsequential and a pawn in the hands of Fortune, wherefore eating and drinking must be the expression of life (34 and 55), that the world turns like a mill, bringing evil to man (39), that a man should pay as much attention to the appointments of his tomb as of his temporary home (71), and that money is the measure of man (77); but his crowning expression is the anti-philosophical statement in his epitaph, in which he boasts that he "never listened to a philosopher" (71). His coarseness also reveals itself in the level of his humor: he takes delight in base and ludicrous situations, his absolutely atrocious puns (e.g. *Carpe, Carpe – "Carve 'er, Carver"* – chap. 36; *Dionyse, Liber esto* – see note on 41b) are immensely gratifying to his boorish sense of humor, the kinds of entertainment that please and amuse him would hardly find a place in the home of the well-bred Roman, and every expression of his lips, humorous, mock-serious and serious, epitomizes his inferior breeding. In spite of all this – his coarseness, his buffoonery, his ostentation, his arrogance, in short, his absurdity – it is difficult not to admire and sympathize with him, so successful is Petronius' characterization. This parody of extravagance shows the skillfulness of the author, who controls the narration and the dialogue with such genial humor and such grace that even the vulgar and bombastic Trimalchio interests and amuses us rather than offending and insulting us, with the result that it is possible to become so involved in the characters of the story that the caricature and the satire can almost catch us off our guard. This is a tribute to the genius of Petronius which is bound to be extracted from all but the most unsympathetic and unappreciative reader.

Fortunata is a fitting mate for Trimalchio, and Petronius' characterization of her is handled with superb artistry, almost surpassing his portraiture of Trimalchio. The first description of her comes from the lips of one of the guests early in the banquet (37); it serves as a brief, anticipatory introduction,

presenting a skeletal figure to be fleshed out later in the
course of the narrative but providing the clear framework for
subsequent characterization. When asked to identify the
woman bustling about the room, Encolpius' neighbor informs
him that she is Fortunata, the host's wife, and offers this
thumb-nail sketch: her name suits her well, for she counts her
money like grain — by the bushel — although not long ago her
station in life (as a prostitute) was so lowly that one would
have hesitated even to accept a piece of bread from her; she
has Trimalchio wrapped around her little finger and, while he
doesn't know the extent of his own wealth, she keeps her eye
on everything; besides, she is a penny-pincher, never drinks
and has a good head on her shoulders; her fault is her tongue
and she will henpeck even in bed; there is no doubt, however,
about her friends and foes, for she does not mask her feelings.
When Habinnas and Scintilla arrive, he observes Fortunata's
absence from the dinner party and asks an explanation (67).
Trimalchio's reply reinforces the earlier sketch: she won't
touch even a drop of water until she has supervised the storing
of the silver and the division of the left-overs among the
slaves; clearly, she wants to be sure that no slave gets more
than his due or has a chance to pilfer any silver to save
toward the price of purchasing his freedom. Obviously fond of
her, Habinnas threatens to leave unless she joins them at
once. The description of her appearance and her apparel adds
further touches to the portrait: she is gaudily dressed, right
down to the heavy ankle ornaments and gold-embroidered
shoes; her use of a neckerchief as a towel further betrays her
low class, as does her cheap display of affection for Scintilla,
the wife of Habinnas. A deft, but not too subtle, touch is
added with the descriptive remark that she removed the
bracelets *crassissimis lacertis,* "from her grotesquely fat
arms," to show them off to Scintilla, who is her near equal in
the competition of vulgar display. They chatter on, giggling
and exchanging low-brow boasts in an effort to outdo each
other. Habinnas' boorish horseplay (one could hardly dignify
it by calling it flirtation), however, does cause her to blush,
perhaps because it was a brutal reminder of her former tawdry

25

existence. As the festivities go on, the spirit of the occasion
so infects the two women that Fortunata is eager to dance,
while Scintilla's clapping outstrips her chatter (70). The
opportunity apparently is delayed by Trimalchio's digression
on his will – with Fortunata as his sole heir – and the blue-
print for his extravagant and monumental tomb; his tears at the
conclusion of the reading of his epitaph elicit wails from
Fortunata and sympathetic sobs from the entire household
(71-72). After an intermission at the baths, the party resumes
in another dining room where Fortunata has laid out some of
her prize possessions for the guests to admire. The peace
and harmony between Trimalchio and Fortunata suddenly is
disrupted by her jealousy at his prolonged kissing of his pet
slave; she hurls a volley of degrading insults until the enraged
Trimalchio retaliates, slamming a wine goblet into her face
and shouting that he has foolishly changed her from a slut to a
respectable woman when he could have married a wealthy
heiress; in a final burst of fury he instructs Habinnas to remove her statue from his tomb and announces that she is even
to be denied the privilege of kissing his corpse. The intervention of Habinnas and Scintilla reduces this volatile fellow
to tears of remorse and self-pity, but then his anger flares up
again; no reconciliation is recorded in the story, although there
appears to be a softening of Trimalchio's ire. At any rate,
Petronius leaves us with a revealing portrait of her: raised
from a slum existence to a position of wealth and power in
Trimalchio's home, she is degraded and humiliated because of
her jealousy and voluble tongue, as well as Trimalchio's
temper. Her dreams shattered, her status within the family
stripped away, all that remains is the shallowness of character typical of the chorus girl who cannot be converted by
wealth alone into a lady.

The other guests at the banquet are more quickly sketched,
but with equal attention to realistic detail; Trimalchio is
painted larger than life, like the fresco on his wall, but the
rest are sketched, as it were, in cameo or at least in a small
etching. For example, the guest who described Fortunata and
some of the guests for Encolpius (37) reveals his character

through his comments about others: his set of values corresponds to those of his wealth-oriented comrades at Trimalchio's tables; he is impressed by the evidences of Trimalchio's wealth, by Diogenes' advertisement of his apartment for rent because he is buying a country estate, by the cleverness of Proculus, the undertaker who made and lost a fortune, but concealed his financial reverses from his creditors by advertising his *spare* furnishings for sale. He is the kind of person who would gawk in unrestrained admiration and envy at any display of wealth, the type of individual who would be unable to conceal his uneasiness in the presence of his social superiors; we need not look far to find him in any society.

Dama, Seleucus, Phileros, Ganymedes and Echion are all briefly but realistically sketched during the scene when Trimalchio is temporarily absent from the table (41-46). From them flows a steady stream of idle gossip, stock phrases and arm-chair aphorisms, but each is distinct from the other, clearly drawn by the expert portrait painter. Dama is drunk, and admits it with perfect candor but imperfect syntax – at once an indication of his character and his condition; nonetheless, his integrity endears him to the reader. Seleucus is equally forthright, but more dogmatic and opinionated. His brief monologue on life and death, doctors, funerals and women is delightfully amusing, and his remark about doctors offers a priceless quotation: "A doctor is good for nothing except peace of mind." Our narrator and his comrades soon tire of him, however, and our attention is diverted to Phileros, whose straightforward descriptions of the dead Chrysanthus and his brother are as revelatory of his own character as of those whom he describes: he both envied and admired Chrysanthus for the wealth he acquired but he prefers his brother who is generous with what little he has; he gives grudging praise to Chrysanthus for his success in business, attributing it to luck, and strongly condemns Chrysanthus for disinheriting his own kin; on one account, however, he is unreserved in his praise, lauding the dead man for his continued virility even in his old age.

Ganymedes is politically and religiously conservative, he

is nostalgic about the good old days when bread was cheap, politicians were kept honest by a high-minded and active citizenry, old Safinius spoke out forcefully, directly and concisely in the Assembly, women were purehearted and men were religiously devout; but now he is pessimistic about everything, for in contemporary society he observes the reverse of all the old moral, political and religious virtues. Echion, the rag-seller, on the other hand, is a relativist and an optimist; he expects luck to change, he anticipates with obvious relish the approaching gladiatorial show and he delights in sharing the gossip about an affair involving Glyco's wife and his steward. But Echion is also sensitive about his inferior education and, with a hint of paranoia, presumes to divine that Agamemnon is harboring disdain for these poor men and their uncultured conversation; he has, however, high hopes for a good but practical education for his son, much like the factory worker in 20th-century America.

It would be possible to describe the character of other figures (especially the individualized slaves) who appear more or less briefly on the scene, but it is sufficient to remark that Petronius paints the lower strata of Roman society most realistically and that he vividly and kaleidoscopically captures their seemingly infinite variations. Loudness, lewdness, cheap sentimentality, fawning obsequiousness, and almost every other possible expression of human behavior is depicted with a freshness and a lack of duplication that is at once praiseworthy and surprising. Petronius reveals a keen awareness of human psychology and the Roman sense for individual uniqueness demonstrated in so much of Roman portrait sculpture. This accounts for the realism and vividness of the characters portrayed in the *Satyricon* and, in particular, in its excerpt, the *Cena*.

THE STYLE: VARIETY WITH INTEGRITY

Versatility, sensitivity and realism characterize not only the human portraiture in the *Satyricon,* but become especially apparent in Petronius' style. The stylistic variations even in the *Cena* are sufficiently numerous to demonstrate Petronius' integrity and accuracy of control over every shift in style; the slips, the inconsistencies, the unintentional blunders of the amateur are all absent, while the master artist's creativity and ingenuity are everywhere obvious but unobtrusive. The author's choice of a word or phrase is always consistent with the role and status of the character involved, whether he is engaged in descriptive narration, table talk or literary criticism; the most minute detail demanded by internal consistency is never ignored, never overlooked. Petronius assumes, as it were, the very character of the person he is portraying, with the result that the individual's mannerisms of thought and expression are presented with precision and ingenuity.

The deliberateness of Petronius' stylistic techniques is at times almost overwhelming. The barbarisms and vulgarities of expression that once were emended by well-meaning but unenlightened textual critics are now recognized as intentional mistakes adapted to the character and social position of the person speaking. The absence of an individual's linguistic and literary elegance is indicative of his lack of social (and sometimes moral) refinement. Idiosyncrasies of style arise from personal peculiarities deliberately and artfully depicted by an author who is almos　unique among his contemporaries in his ability to appreciate not only the refined elegance of Silver Age Latin, but even the many bastardized vulgarisms of the everyday conversations of the uneducated masses.

The correctness of diction and stylistic elegance of Encolpius and Agamemnon stands in sharp contrast with the talk of freedmen like Trimalchio and his friends at the banquet, for their speech reveals a paucity of education resulting in vulgarisms and colloquialisms, and even in obvious blunders of grammar and syntax. Thus the narrative passages are felicitous, fresh and vigorous in their style, while the conversation at Trimalchio's table is filled with the slang and solecisms, cliches and outworn aphorisms of the hybrid population of Campania. The author is at once involved in his characters and at the same time aloof from them, thus contributing through this moral detachment a spirit of gentle irony and satire that amuses the reader while also arousing his admiration.

Trimalchio's speech is often bombastic, but he speaks with an openness and self-satisfaction characteristic of a self-made millionaire. He can be insensitive to and unconcerned about the reactions of his better-educated guests, for they owe their meal and their entertainment to him. His own financial success, moreover, makes him pompous and imperious, traits reflected in his speech. His language is the *lingua Romana rustica,* the popular country speech of southern Italy.[13] Because of the original Greek character of this region of Italy, the language of Trimalchio and his comrades abounds in such Grecisms as the use of a neuter plural with a singular verb *(faciatur . . . et triclinia,* 71c) and numerous Greek words.[14] Just as Trimalchio confused his myths and legends, so also he confuses his syntax: genders are mixed *(malus fatus* for *malum fatum,* 71a, and *fatus meus* for *fatum meum,* 77b), he makes a transitive verb into a deponent *(me fastiditum,* 48b), multiplies his negatives *(nemini tamen nihil satis est,* 76a), changes conjugations *(defraudit* for *defraudat,* 69a) and is guilty of various other irregularities in the conjugation of verbs and in his omission of connecting particles (called asyndeton), common faults in the casual conversation of the uneducated.

His poorly educated friends also commit frequent syntactical blunders. Echion similarly mixes genders *(libra rubricata* for *libros rubricatos,* 46c; *thesaurum* for *thesaurus,* 46d) and uses syntax common only to vulgar and late Latin *(dixi quod,* 46b; *litterae thesaurum est,* 46d; and *te persuadeam,* 46a). Dama and Seleucus likewise garble their genders *(balneus,* 41e; *balniscus,* 42a; and *malus fatus,* 42b – in each case the mas-

---

[13]Cf. the introduction to the translation of the *Satyricon* ascribed to Oscar Wilde (New York, 1934).

[14]Cf. William E. Waters, *Petronius Cena Trimalchionis* (Boston, 1902), index p. 141 *(s.v.* "Greek words") for a fairly complete list. Examples include *chiramaxium* (28a), *paronychia* (31b) *lasanum* (41d) and *bybliotheca* (48b).

culine displaces the neuter of literary Latin) and Niceros uses the accusative in place of the dative case *(persuadeo hospitem,* 62a).

Besides these frequent instances of the speech of the common people *(sermo plebeius)* are certain other features representative of the conversations of people from the lower strata of society. One of these is the frequent interposing of popular sayings and proverbs, such as:

aqua dentes habet (42a)
antiquus amor cancer est (42c)
serva me, servabo te (44a)
urceatim plovebat (44f)
non est miscix (45b)
Ille milvo volanti poterat ungues resecare (45c)
colubra restem non parit (45c)
sibi quisque peccat (45c)
manus manum lavat (45d)
quicquid discis, tibi discis (46d)
litterae thesaurum est (46d)
artificium numquam moritur (46d)
qualis est dominus, talis et servus (58a)
qui vincitur, vincit (59a).

With the exception of the last saying, all are uttered by Trimalchio's *colliberti,* and all but one of the rest are woven into the fabric of their conversation during Trimalchio's absence from the table. This appears to be a deliberate technique employed by Petronius to accentuate the homogeneity of these common folk through their stock phrases and ready cliches, while he also is careful to give each one an individual flavor to distinguish him from the next.

In general, the coarseness of the speech, combined with an unconcerned forthrightness, distinguishes Trimalchio's comrades from Agamemnon, Encolpius and his friends, but there also is a certain flavor to Trimalchio's speech that sets him apart from both groups. The ease with which Petronius moves back and forth from the style of one character to that of another and to the fluency of the narrative description reveals

31

his great genius. The purity of his style and the authenticity of his characterization combine to produce a most pleasurable experience for the reader, an experience that is heightened by the light and gentle humor of Petronius' penetrating and pervasive satire.

THE SCHOLARS: A HIGHLY SELECTIVE BIBLIOGRAPHY

This bibliography is intentionally very limited in scope and is designed to provide only a starting point for the reader who wishes to explore some aspect of Petronian scholarship that interests him. It includes only a few of the titles that proved useful or interesting to me in the preparation of this introduction.

Complete Texts

Buecheler, Franz. *Petronii Saturae*. Berlin, 1958.
Ernout, Alfred. *Pétrone, Le Satiricon*. ed. 3. Paris, 1950.

Annotated Editions

Friedlaender, Ludwig. *Petronii Cena Trimalchionis*. Leipzig, 1906 (repr. Amsterdam, 1960).
Sedgwick, W. B. *The Cena Trimalchionis, together with Seneca's Apocolocyntosis and a selection of Pompeian inscriptions*. ed. 2. Oxford, 1950.
Waters, William E. *Petronius, Cena Trimalchionis*. Boston, 1902.

Translations

Arrowsmith, William. *Petronius, The Satyricon*. Ann Arbor, 1959 (also published as a Mentor Classic paperback).
Lindsay, Jack. *The Complete Works of Gaius Petronius, with one hundred illustrations by Norman Lindsay*. New York, 1932.
Wilde, Oscar (ascribed to). *The Satyricon of Petronius Arbiter*. New York, 1934

General Works

Bagnani, Gilbert. *Arbiter of Elegance: A Study of the Life & Works of C. Petronius.* Toronto, 1954 (*Phoenix* Suppl. Vol. II).

Carcopino, Jerome. *Daily Life in Ancient Rome,* transl. by E. O. Lorimer, ed. by Henry T. Rowell. New Haven, 1940.

Marmorale, Enzo V. *La Questione Petroniana.* Bari, 1948.

Stefenelli, Arnulf. *Die Volkssprache im Werk des Petron.* Stuttgart, 1962.

Todd, F. A. *Some Ancient Novels.* London, 1940.

PREFACE TO THE
FIRST EDITION

The purpose of this book is to provide a readable unit of
Latin for college students at the intermediate level. The
raison d'être for the kind of book here presented is set forth in
my article, "Word Count Editing of Latin Texts," *Classical
Journal* for November 1954.

The form of the book does not necessarily imply any pref-
erence in teaching method, but both teacher and student may
use it more effectively by keeping in mind the observations
below.

The text is a fair sample of the Latinity of Petronius. Except for a few transitional phrases, the grammar, syntax, idiom,
sentence structure, and word order are presented as in a
standard text. Vocabulary density, however, has been con-
siderably reduced by the omission of a few episodes, compres-
sion of certain detailed descriptions, and in some cases, sub-
stitution of synonyms drawn mainly from Petronius' own
vocabulary. Thus the text is not, in the usual sense of the
terms, adapted or expurgated; it retains the essential flavor
of Petronius.

Vocabulary falls under three heads:

(1) Words *assumed* are those most commonly used in elementary Latin, plus others obviously related to them or to everyday English words.

(2) Words *assigned* are those used several times in the text, most of which are fairly common in general. Each of these is given in the notes the first time it occurs; it is marked with an asterisk to indicate that it is an item to be added to the student's working vocabulary.

(3) Words *noted* are given in the notes for every passage in which they occur.

The vocabulary list at the end of the book contains only the words assumed and assigned, the latter marked with asterisks. Thus whenever the student finds it necessary to consult the vocabulary, he can be sure that the word in question is either an elementary word, a related word, or a word he should have learned with a previous assignment; in short, it is a word he might reasonably be expected to know. The intelligent student will minimize the thumbing of pages by making a point of memorizing the principal parts and meanings of every assigned word as it occurs. It is suggested that the student make a list of all words he has to look up for each assignment and review them every day until he is sure that he has mastered them.

In the written exercises the student is to use, as far as possible, words and structures found in the preceding reading assignments. Before attempting a given exercise, he will save time and frustration by carefully re-reading the passage on which it is based, reviewing the vocabulary and pining down the grammar.

The *Cena Trimalchionis* is the story of a wild dinner party, given by Trimalchio, the most pretentious parvenu ever imagined. It is part of the so-called *Satyricon,* a sort of sociological caricature, written apparently by Petronius, a super-sophisticated satirist, in the time of the incredible Emperor Nero (54-68 A.D.). Ordinary curiosity will intrigue most students into searching the library for more complete background material and fuller interpretation.[1] To begin with, however, the following may suffice.

The relationships of the characters are self-explanatory, except for

Encólpius, the young man who tells the tale
Ascýltos, his buddy
Gíton, a young boy, who for the moment is acting as slave
    to Encolpius and Ascyltos
Agamémnon, their teacher
Meneláus, friend to Agamemnon

The situation at the beginning of the *Cena* (because of the fragmentary condition of the manuscripts) is somewhat obscure. Apparently Encolpius and Ascyltos have got themselves into some sort of predicament in some Italian town (possibly Cumae) and are vainly trying to plan their escape, when they are reminded by a message from Agamemnon that they are invited to a dinner party at Trimalchio's.

The social background is rather complex. Except for Trimalchio, the characters above mentioned are *liberi,* free men, with full rights of Roman citizenship. Trimalchio and his other guests are *liberti,* freedmen, i.e. ex-slaves, who have been granted limited citizenship. They are very proud of their successful "social mobility," sometimes refer to each other as *colliberti,* fellow-freedmen, and never miss an opportunity to impress upon others, especially upon slaves, the importance of their newly acquired social privileges.

A *servus,* slave, became a *libertus* through manumission *(manu + mittere),* a legal process by which the *dominus,* master, renounced his ownership of the slave. The master then became *patronus,* patron, of the new freedman, and the latter became his *cliens,* client. Each of them was still under certain minor obligations to the other.

---

[1]The present edition owes most to the editions of Bücheler, Friedländer, Waters, and Sedgwick.

Students will enrich their appreciation of the text by exploring standard reference books on these and other points of Roman social and private life.

Reproduction of this experimental edition was made possible through a grant from the University Research Committee of Wayne State University.

May 1960   Thomas Cutt

THE CENA TRIMALCHIONIS
OF PETRONIUS

Venerat jam tertius dies, id est expectatio liberae   26a
cenae, sed tot vulneribus confossis fuga magis placebat
quam quies. Itaque cum maesti deliberaremus quonam
genere praesentem evitaremus procellam, unus servus
Agamemnonis interpellavit trepidantes et "Quid? Vos,"
inquit, "nescitis hodie apud quem fiat? Trimalchio,
lautissimus homo, horologium in triclinio et bucinatorem

26a

*cēna ae f, dinner, dinner party
confossis (supply *nobis*), to us
    (who were) riddled − The
    "wounds" with which our
    heroes were riddled apparently
    were some troubles that made
    them prefer to get away *(fuga)*
    rather than to stay put *(quies)*.
maesti, gloomily
quonam genere, how in the world
procellam (acc.), storm
Agamemnon onis − See page 37.

interpellavit (supply *nos*) trepi-
    dantes, broke in upon our panic
Quid, Hey
*nēsciō īre īvī, not know
*hodiē, today
apud quem fiat, who's throwing a
    party
Trimalchio onis − See page 37.
*lautus a um, washed, elegant,
    swell − See *lavō* in vocabulary.
horologium, clock
*trīclīnium ī n, dining room
bucinatorem (acc.), trumpeter

39

habet subornatum, ut subinde sciat quantum de vita perdiderit.''

Amicimur ergo diligenter, obliti omnium malorum, et   26b
Gitona, libentissime servi officium tuentem usque hoc,
jubemus in balnea sequi.

subornatum (acc.), in a smart uniform	*ergō, therefore, so; then, well!
*subinde, repeatedly	*oblīvīscor ī oblītus (+ gen.), forget
*perdō ere perdidi perditus, lose ruin	Gitona (acc.) — See page 37.
	*libenter, gladly
	usque hoc, still
26b	*balneum ī n, bath, bath room —
	Public baths *(balnea)* were used like modern clubhouses for
Amicimur, we got dressed	games, etc.

Written Exercise 26 — See Introduction p. 36.

Write in Latin:

1 So I did not know who these elegant gentlemen were.
2 I shall gladly come to dinner at your house *(apud tē)* today.
3 He repeatedly told us to forget all (our) troubles.
4 You did not know at whose house the dinner party was to take place?
5 The boys knew who had followed (them) into the (public) bath.
6 Come into the dining room; don't ruin the dinner!

Nos interim errare coepimus et circulis ludentium   27a
accedere, cum subito videmus senem calvum, tunica
vestitum russea, inter pueros capillatos ludentem pila.

	senem . . . russea, a bald old gentleman, dressed in a red tunic
27a	
*errō āre āvī ātus, wander about, be mistaken	*tunica ae f, tunic
circulis (dat. with *accedere*), groups	*capillātus a um, long-haired — It was the height of luxury to have young, long-haired slave boys for personal service.
ludo ere, play (games)	

40

Nec tam pueri nos ad spectaculum duxerant quam ipse
pater familiae, qui soleatus pila prasina exercebatur.
Nec amplius pilam repetebat quae terram contigerat, sed
follem plenum habebat servus sufficiebatque ludentibus.

Cum has ergo miraremur lautitias, accurrit Menelaus;   27b
"Hic est," inquit, "apud quem cubitum ponetis, et
quidem jam principium cenae videtis." Et jam non
loquebatur Menelaus cum Trimalchio digitos concrepuit
et aquam poposcit ad manus. Tunc digitos paululum
sparsos in capite pueri tersit.

---

pila ae f, ball
soleatus, in his slippers
prasinus a um, green
*contingo ere tigi tāctus, touch,
  happen
follem (acc.), a bag
*plēnus a um, full, bountiful, full
  spread
sufficiebat, supplied (fresh balls)

27b

*lautitia ae f (cp. *lautus*),

elegance, luxury
Menelaus – See page 37.
cubitum ponere, to prop one's
  elbow, i.e. to recline, to dine –
  The Romans reclined at meals.
principium, preliminaries
*digitus ī m, finger
concrepuit, snapped
*tunc, then, at that time
paululum, for a mere moment
*spargo ere sī sus, sprinkle,
  scatter, spatter
*tergeo ēre sī sus, wipe

Written Exercise 27 – See Introduction p. 36.

Write in Latin:

1 Full of expectation, we were wandering about in the bath, when
   suddenly we saw some long-haired slave boys.
2 They were admiring some tunics, which they began to touch with
   their hands.
3 So when we were talking about these luxuries, Trimalchio himself
   came into the bath.
4 He sprinkled some water on the ground with his fingers.
5 Then he began to wipe his hands on the head of a long-haired
   slave boy.

41

Nos intravimus balneum, et sudore calfacti momento 28a
temporis ad frigidam eximus. Jam Trimalchio unguento
perfusus tergebatur, non linteis, sed palliis ex lana
mollissima factis. Hinc involutus coccina gausapa lecticae impositus est, praecedentibus phaleratis cursoribus
quattuor et chiramaxio, in quo deliciae ejus vehebantur,
puer vetulus, lippus, domino Trimalchione deformior.

Cum ergo auferretur, ad caput ejus symphoniacus cum 28b
minimis tibiis accessit, et tamquam in aurem aliquid
secreto diceret, toto itinere cantavit.

Sequimur nos admiratione jam pleni, et cum Agamem- 28c
none ad januam pervenimus, in cujus poste libellus erat
cum hac inscriptione fixus: "Quisquis servus sine dominico jussu foras exierit, accipiet plagas centum." Super

---

28a

*intrō āre āvī ātus, enter
sudore calfacti, heated up with a
good sweat
frigidam (aquam), the cold water —
They plunged directly from the
hot pool into the cold one, without entering the intermediate,
warm pool, as was customary.
*unguentum ī n, perfume
*perfundō ere fūdī fūsus, pour
over, drench
linteis, with linen towels
palliis, with blankets
*lāna ae f, wool
mollissima (abl.), very soft
*hinc (cp. *hic*), from this point,
then, next
*involvō, ere vī ūtus, roll up,
wrap up
coccina gausapa, in a scarlet
woolen cloak
lecticae (dat. with *impositus*), on
a litter
phaleratis cursoribus (abl.), foot-
men in gaudy livery
chiramaxio (abl.), a hand waggon
deliciae, pet slave boy — Lit. delights (plural).

vetulus, shriveled up
lippus, blear-eyed
*dominus ī m, master
deformior, uglier

28b

*auferō auferre abstulī ablātus,
carry away, remove, take away
symphoniacus (nom.), musician
tibiis (abl. pl.), flute
*tamquam, as much as, as, as if,
just like
*auris is f, ear
*cantō āre āvī ātus, make music,
sing, play

28c

*jānua ae f, door
poste (abl.), jamb, doorpost
libellus, placard
inscriptione, notice
*quisquis quicquid, whoever,
whatever
dominico jussu (abl.), the
master's permission
foras, out of the house
plagas (acc.), lashes
*super (+ acc.), above, over, on
top of, next (at table)

januam autem cavea pendebat argentea, in qua pica
intrantes salutabat.

---

cavea, cage	pica, magpie
*argenteus a um, silver	salutabat, greeted

Written Exercise 28

1 Whatever you have, give (it) to me.
2 Don't bandage your finger with wool.
3 I see that you have a tunic made of wool.
4 I don't like perfume. Take it away!
5 Above the door of the dining room there was a silver figurine
(*statunculum* n.).
6 With my own ears I have repeatedly heard your master singing in
the bath room.
7 Then some slaves, drenched with perfume, entered the dining room
and began to sing, as if ordered (to do so) by their master.

Ceterum ego dum omnia stupeo, paene resupinatus   29a
crura mea fregi. Ad sinistram enim intrantibus canis
ingens, catena vinctus, in pariete erat pictus, superque
quadrata littera scriptum "Cave canem!" Et socii
quidem mei riserunt.

Ego autem collecto spiritu non destiti totum parietem   29b
persequi. Erat autem venalicium cum titulis pictum, et
ipse Trimalchio capillatus caduceum tenebat, Minervaque

29a

*cēterum, but, besides
stupeo, I was gawking at
paene . . . fregi, I just about
  toppled over backwards and
  broke my legs
*canis is m or f, dog
*ingēns entis, great, huge
catena vinctus, on a leash
paries etis m. wall
*pingō ere pinxi pictus, paint,
  depict
quadrata littera, in large capitals
cave, beware of
*rideō ēre rīsī rīsus, laugh,
  laugh at

29b

collecto spiritu, recovering my
  breath
venalicium cum titulis, a sale of
  slaves, with advertisements —
  Prices and qualities of slaves
  were posted up on placards,
  just like display cards in a
  modern store.
caduceum (acc.), the emblem of
  Mercury — Mercury was patron
  god of business men (and
  thieves).
Minerva, goddess of know-how —
  The frescoes mean that
  Trimalchio, originally a slave

43

ducente Romam intrabat. Hinc quemadmodum ratiocinari
didicisset, denique dispensator factus esset, omnia
diligenter curiosus pictor cum inscriptione reddiderat.
Interrogare ergo atriensem coepi, quas in medio pic-   29c
turas haberent. "Iliada et Odyssian," inquit, "ac
Laenatis gladiatorium munus."

Nos jam ad triclinium perveneramus, sed cum   30a
conaremur intrare, exclamavit unus ex pueris, qui super
hoc officium erat positus, "Dextro pede!" Sine dubio
paulisper veriti sumus ne contra praeceptum aliquis
nostrum limen transiret. Ceterum ut pariter movimus
dextros gressus, servus nobis despoliatus se projecit
ad pedes ac rogare coepit, ut se poenae eriperemus:
nec magnum esse peccatum suum, propter quod periclitaretur;

---

boy *(capillatus)*, with the help
of the gods gained Roman
citizenship and made a fortune.
*quemadmodum, how, as
*discō ere didicī, learn
ratiocinari, to do bookkeeping
*dēnique, finally
dispensator (nom.), cashier
curiosus pictor (nom.), the pains-
taking painter
cum inscriptione, with a descriptive caption (for each picture)

29c

atriensem (acc.), the major-domo
Iliada . . . munus, "Frescoes of
scenes from the *Iliad* and
Odyssey," said he, "and the
gladiatorial games of Laenas."

30a

Dextro pede: supply *intrate* −
English idiom for this?
Sine dubio, naturally
contra praeceptum, without ob-
serving the rule − i.e. left foot
first, which was a bad omen.
limen (acc.), threshold
pariter, in unison − Like goose-
stepping soldiers.
gressus = pedes − Poetic idiom,
here whimsical.
despoliatus (nom.), stripped (for
a flogging)
ut . . . eriperemus, that we
rescue; i.e. us to rescue
nec . . . esse: supply *dixit* − N.B.
An indirect statement may de-
pend upon a verbal idea which
is merely implied by the context.
peccatum (acc.), offense
periclitaretur = in periculo esset

subducta enim sibi vestimenta dispensatoris in balneo,
quae vix fuissent decem sestertiorum.

Rettulimus ergo dextros pedes, dispensatoremque in   30b
atrio aureos numerantem deprecati sumus ut servo remit-
teret poenam. Superbus ille sustulit vultum et, "Non
tam jactura me movet," inquit, "quam negligentia nequis-
simi servi. Vestimenta mea cubitoria perdidit, quae mihi
natali meo cliens quidam donaverat, Tyria sine dubio, sed
jam semel lauta. Quid ergo est? Dono vobis eum."

---

subducta (esse), had been
  snitched
*vestīmentum ī n, garment; pl.
  clothes
dispensator oris m, cashier —
  The *dispensator* is probably a
  libertus (See page 37), who has
  reached the higher echelons of
  Trimalchio's huge household
  (familia). When he goes to the
  baths, he has a slave attend him
  (as a fine gentleman should!) to
  guard his clothes. Since the
  slave has failed in his duty, he
  will have him flogged, to prove
  he knows how to act like the
  fine gentleman he thinks he has
  become.
decem sestertiorum, worth ten
  sesterces — No great amount of
  money in a house rolling in
  wealth.

*aureus ī m, gold coin
deprecati sumus, we begged
Superbus, haughtily
*vultus ūs m, face, countenance,
  glance
non tam — quam: cp. 27a, Nec
  tam pueri — quam pater familiae
jactura ae f, loss
nequissimus a um, good-for-
  nothing
cubitoria (with *vestimenta),*
  dinner clothes
natali meo, on my birthday
dono are, give (as a gift)
Tyria sine dubio, Tyrian purple,
  of course — An expensive fabric.
*semel, once
*lavo are lavi lautus, wash,
  bathe, launder; passive, take a
  bath
Quid . . . eum, So what? You can
  have him. — Literally?

30b

atrio (abl.), the living room

Written Exercise 29, 30

1 They did not know how he had become a slave.
2 Besides, as I entered the dining room, I saw a huge dog with a
  very sad *(maestus a um)* face.
3 He finally learned to paint.
4 He begged us not to laugh.
5 Because I had once done (so), she repeatedly tried to persuade me
  to launder the clothes myself.
6 The slave begged us to give him five gold coins.

Obligati tam grandi beneficio cum intrassemus tri- **31a**
clinium, occurrit nobis ille idem servus pro quo rogaveramus,
et stupentibus spississima basia impegit, gratias agens
humanitati nostrae. "Ad summam, statim scietis," ait,
"cui dederitis beneficium. Vinum dominicum ministratoris
gratia est."

Tandem ergo discubuimus, pueris Alexandrinis aquam **31b**
in manus nivatam infundentibus, aliisque insequentibus
ad pedes ac paronychia cum ingenti subtilitate tollentibus.
Ac ne in hoc quidem tam molesto tacebant officio, sed
obiter cantabant. Ego experiri volui an tota familia
cantaret. Itaque potionem poposci. Paratissimus puer
non minus me acido cantico excepit. Et quisquis aliquid
rogatus erat ut daret semper cantans dabat.

Jam omnes discubuerant praeter ipsum Trimalchionem, **31c**
cum allata est gustatio valde lauta. In promulsidari

31a

stupentibus . . . nostrae, to our
amazement he forced upon us
the most lavish kisses *(basia)*,
by way of gratitude for our
kindness to him
*ad summam, in short, 'smatter
of fact
*ajō ais ait ajunt, say, assert
Vinum . . . est, The master's
wine is the butler's gift — i.e.
he will see that they are
served the best wine in the
house.

31b

*discumbō ere cubuī cubitus,
lean, lie, recline (at table)
Alexandrinus a um, Alexandrian
nivatus a um, snow-cooled
*īnfundō ere fūdī fūsus, pour into,
pour over
paronychia tollentibus, trimming
our toenails — Romans removed
their shoes at table.

subtilitate (abl.), finesse
*molestus a um, vexatious, bore-
some
*taceō ēre tacuī tacitus, be silent
obiter, as they worked — Literally?
tota familia, all the slaves —
Familia has three meanings:
1, family, as in normal English;
2, household, including mem-
bers of the family *and* the
slaves; 3, the slaves, as here.
*pōtiō ōnis f, a drink
*parātus a um, ready, prompt
acido (with *cantico*), shrill
*canticum ī n, singing, song
me excepit, took me up on it

31c

gustatio (nom.), the appetizer
*valdē, very, very much
In promulsidari . . . positus, On
a hors d'oeuvre tray there was
a Corinthian bronze donkey
served up with a pair of
panniers

46

asellus erat Corinthius cum bisaccio positus, qui habebat
olivas, in altera parte albas, in altera nigras. Ceterum
duae lances, in quarum marginibus nomen Trimalchionis
inscriptum erat et argenti pondus, continebant glires
melle ac papavere sparsos.

---

*albus a um, white; here, green
*niger gra grum, black; here, ripe
lances (nom.), platters
*argentum ī n, silver

pondus (nom.), weight
glires (acc.) dormice
melle ac papavere, with honey
and poppy seed

Written Exercise 31

1 Boresome (people) never will learn to be silent.
2 When all (the guests) had reclined (at table), the slaves began to
  sing a very boresome song.
3 The boy was very prompt, but I begged him not to pour any water
  into my drink.
4 He begged them to give him the silver.
5 In short, I assert that these men had white tunics, not black.

In his eramus lautitiis, cum ipse Trimalchio ad   32
symphoniam allatus est, positusque inter cervicalia minu-
tissima expressit imprudentibus risum. Pallio enim
coccineo adrasum excluserat caput, circaque oneratas
veste cervices laticlaviam immiserat mappam, fimbriis
hinc atque illinc pendentibus. Habebat etiam in minimo

32

*symphōnia ae f, orchestra; ad,
  to the accompaniment of
cervicalia (acc.), cushions
expressit imprudentibus, drew
  from the unwary
*rīsus ūs m, laughter (cp. *rīdeō)
Pallio . . . caput, For his bald pate
  peered out atop a scarlet robe.
  — He was dressed up to the
  ears!

*circā (+ acc.), around
*onerō āre āvī ātus, load
*cervīx īcis f, neck (plural =
  singular) — Cp. cervicalia,
  above.
laticlaviam mappam (acc.), a
  purple-striped table napkin
fimbriis . . . pendentibus, with
  fringe dangling
hinc atque illinc (cp. hic and
  ille), from this point and from
  that, this way and that

digito sinistrae manus anulum grandem subauratum, extre-
mo vero articulo digiti sequentis minorem, ut mihi videbatur, totum aureum.

Ut deinde pinna argentea dentes perfodit. "Amici," 33a
inquit, "nondum mihi suave erat in triclinium venire, sed
ne diutius absentivos morae vobis essem, omnem voluptatem
mihi negavi. Permittetis tamen finiri lusum." Sequebatur
puer cum tabula terebinthina et crystallinis tesseris,
notavique rem omnium delicatissimam: pro calculis enim
albis ac nigris aureos argenteosque habebat denarios.

Interim dum ille omnium textorum dicta inter lusum 33b
consumit, gustantibus adhuc nobis, repositorium allatum est
cum corbe, in quo gallina erat lignea, patentibus in orbem

---

anulum . . . subauratum (acc.),
 an enormous, gold-plated ring
articulus i m, joint
*aureus a um, of gold, gold(en)

33a

pinna (abl.), toothpick
*dēns dentis m, tooth, tusk
perfodit, picked
*suāvis e, pleasant — Diction-
 aries give dignified meanings
 for this word, but in the
 everyday language of this book
 suavis connotes fun or a good
 time. Here we may translate:
 It was no fun for me to come
 right this minute. — Later you
 will find phrases such as
 suaviter facio and *suaviter est
 mihi*, I am having fun, I am
 having a good time.
absentivos = absens — Trimalchio,
 in trying to be impressive,
 uses a low-brow Latin form
 with a Greek ending. Translate: "by my absence," and to
 bring out the silly effect, pro-
 nounce "absence" as if it
 were French.
voluptatem (acc.), pleasure
lusum (acc.), game

tabula . . . tesseris, a chess-
 board of terebinth, and crystal
 men
*notō āre āvī ātus, notice,
 observe
delicatus a um, exquisite
calculis (abl.), tallies, chips
*dēnārius ī m, denarius — The
 silver denarius corresponds
 roughly to a quarter, the gold,
 to a five dollar gold piece.

33b

textorum (gen.) — Probably from
 textor, a weaver, as typical of
 the populace, whose speech
 was coarse and crude; translate: stevedore.
gustantibus (abl.), nibbling on
 hors d'oeuvres
*adhūc, still
*repositōrium ī n, tray — From
 chapter 36, it is clear that
 repositoria were, sometimes at
 least, quite large, fairly deep,
 and fitted with bell covers.
cum corbe, with a basket on it
gallina . . . ova, there was a
 wooden hen, cuddling her wings
 around her, as hens usually do
 when hatching eggs

48

alis, quales esse solent quae incubant ova. Accessere
continuo duo servi et, symphonia strepente, scrutari
paleam coeperunt, erutaque pavonina ova divisere convivis.

---

*continuō, immediately, forthwith	erutaque . . . ova, and when they
strepente (abl.), booming	had fished out some peahen's
scrutari paleam, to poke around	eggs
in the straw	*convīva ae m or f, guest

Written Exercise 32, 33

1 With loud *(māgnus)* laughter all the guests followed him into the dining room at once.
2 Around the boy's neck was a large chain *(catēna ae* f.).
3 He himself will beg us not to load the ships.
4 It seemed to me that the dog's teeth were huge.
5 It's no fun for me to listen to *(audīre)* this orchestra.
6 (While) the guests (were) still laughing, the slaves brought in a third tray.
7 I notice that you still have ten gold denarii.

Jam Trimalchio eadem omnia, lusu intermisso, popos- 34a
cerat feceratque potestatem clara voce, si quis nostrum
iterum vellet mulsum sumere, cum subito signum symphonia
datur et gustatoria pariter a choro cantante rapiuntur.

Ceterum inter tumultum cum forte paropsis argentea 34b
cecidisset et puer jacentem sustulisset, animadvertit
Trimalchio, colaphisque objurgari puerum ac projicere

34a

lusu (abl.), game
iterum, again
mulsum (acc.), cocktail — Made of wine and honey.
gustatoria (nom. pl.), the hors d'oeuvres
pariter, likewise — i.e. with another musical flourish *(chorus).*

34b

paropsis idis f, a dish

jacentem, from the floor — Literally?
colaphis objurgari, to be punished by having his ears cuffed — Which would be done by a *lorarius,* a slave whose job was to flog other slaves. The *puer* is to be punished, not for dropping the dish, but for assuming that Trimalchio would deign to keep a dish that had touched the floor! Fastidious? Remember the balls in Chapter 27?

rursus paropsidem jussit. Insecutus est supellecticarius argentumque inter reliqua purgamenta scopis coepit everrere.

Statim allatae sunt amphorae vitreae diligenter gypsa-   34c
tae, quarum in cervicibus pittacia erant affixa cum hoc titulo: "Falernum Opimianum annorum centum." Dum titulos perlegimus, complosit Trimalchio manus et "Eheu," inquit, "ergo diutius vivit vinum quam homuncio. Quare tangomenas faciamus. Vita vinum est. Verum Opimianum pono. Heri non tam bonum posui, et multo honestiores cenabant."

Potantibus ergo nobis et diligentissime lautitias mi-   34d
rantibus, larvam argenteam attulit servus sic aptatam ut articuli ejus vertebraeque luxatae in omnem partem move-rentur. Hanc cum super mensam semel iterumque abjecisset, ut catenatio mobilis aliquot figuras exprimeret, Trimalchio adjecit:

---

supellecticarius (nom.), a janitor
purgamenta (acc.), trash (scraps of food, etc.)
scopis everrere, to sweep up

34c

*amphora ae f, wine jar
*vitreus a um, (made of) glass
gypsatae, sealed
pittacia (nom.), tags
titulus ī m, inscription
Falernum Opimianum, Falernian, of the vintage of Opimius — The Falernian District pro-duced excellent wine. The vintage of 121 B.C. (the year Opimius was consul) was es-pecially famous. That the label is a phony is indicated by the absurd addition *annorum centum,* as if a given vintage could continue to be a fixed number of years old!
titulos perlegimus, we drank in the full effect of the labels

complosit, clapped loudly
*ēheu or heu, alas, alack, wella-day, dear me!
*vīnum ī n, wine
homuncio (nom.), poor li'l ole man
*quāre, so, therefore; why *(quā + rē)*
tangomenas (acc.), a night of it, fun, whoopee
Heri, yesterday
*honestus a um, respectable
*cēnō āre āvī ātus, dine

34d

Potantibus (abl.), drinking
larvam (acc.), skeleton
sic aptatam . . . luxatae, so de-signed that when its limbs and spine were twisted
*mēnsa ae f, table
iterum, again
catenatio (nom.), contraption
*aliquot, several, a few
exprimeret, took, adopted

50

"Éheu nós miserós! Quam tótus homúncio níl est!
Síc erimús cunctí postquám nos aúferet Órcus.
Érgo vívamús dúm licet ésse bené."

Laudationem ferculum novum est insecutum.   35
"Suadeo," inquit Trimalchio, "cenemus."

Eheu . . . nil est, Alas, what
  pitiful souls we are! Entirely
  nothing is miniature man!
Sic, thus — Like the skeleton!
  Supple?
cuncti, the whole batch of us
*Orcus ī m, god of the lower
  world, hell, death
*bene esse, to have a good time
  — Trimalchio's verse form is a
  crude tristich which was used
  by illiterate people for epi-

taphs. You can get the rhythm
approximately, by stressing
the syllables marked.

35

Laudationem (acc.), our applause
  (for the poem!)
*ferculum ī n, dish, course (of a
  dinner)
*suādeō = persuādeō, urge,
  advise

Written Exercise 34, 35

1 Let's live, let's dine, let's see the wine.
2 We do live, we do dine, we do see wine.
3 While the first course was being served, Trimalchio said, "Alas,
  a man cannot persuade Orcus (dative) to forget (him)."
4 We have several tables but no (nūllus) trays.
5 They say that respectable Romans began to dine before nightfall
  (nox).
6 I observed that our friend had glass wine jars.
7 Therefore let's persuade them to dine with us while we still have
  (some) good wine.

Haec ut dixit, ad symphoniam quattuor pueri tripudian-   36a
tes procurrerunt, superioremque partem repositorii abstu-
lerunt. Quo facto, videmus altilia et sumina leporemque
in medio pinnis subornatum, ut Pegasus videretur. Nota-

36a

tripudiantes (nom.), dancing
altilia . . . subornatum, plump
  chickens, sows' udders and, in

the middle, a rabbit fitted up
  with wings
Pegasus: the winged horse of
  Bellerophon

vimus etiam circa angulos repositorii Marsyas quattuor,
ex quorum utriculis garum piperatum currebat super pisces,
qui tamquam in euripo natabant. Damus omnes plausum a
familia inceptum, et res electissimas ridentes aggredimur.

    Non minus et Trimalchio ejusmodi methodio laetus,   36b
"Carpe!" inquit. Processit statim scissor, et ad symphoniam gesticulatus, ita laceravit obsonium ut putares
essedarium hydraule cantante pugnare. Iterabat nihilo
minus Trimalchio lentissima voce, "Carpe, Carpe!"

    Ego suspicatus ad aliquam urbanitatem totiens iteratam 36c
vocem pertinere, non dubitavi eum qui supra me discumbebat hoc ipsum interrogare. At ille, qui saepius ejusmodi ludos spectaverat, "Vides illum," inquit, "qui
obsonium carpit? Carpus vocatur. Itaque quotienscumque
dicit 'Carpe,' eodem verbo et vocat et imperat."

---

angulos (acc.), corners
Marsyas, figurines of Marsyas
  (the satyr)
utriculis (abl.), pudgy little
  paunches — Cp. the Manneken-
  Pis in Brussels.
garum piperatum (nom.), pepper
  sauce
*piscis is m, fish
euripo (abl.), a moat
natabant, were as if *(tamquam)*
  swimming — See on *repositorium,*
  33b.
*plausus ūs m, applause
res electissimas (acc.), this
  choice food

36b

*ejusmodī, this sort of, that kind
  of
methodio (abl.), trick
laetus (nom.), delighted
Carpe, Carver, Cutter, Cutt

scissor, a carver — A slave especially trained to carve or
  slice food.
*lacerō āre āvī ātus, lacerate, cut
  to pieces, butcher, carve
obsonium (acc.), victuals
essedarium . . . pugnare, that he
  was a gladiator in a chariot,
  fighting to the music of a water
  organ
itero are avi atus, repeat (over
  over)
lentissima (abl.), drawling

36c

urbanitatem (acc.), something
  clever
totiens, so many times
ludos (acc.), performances
carpit, is carving
quotienscumque, whenever, every
  time

52

Non potui amplius quicquam gustare, sed conversus   37a
ad eum, coepi interrogare quae esset mulier illa quae huc
atque illuc discurreret. "Uxor," inquit, "Trimalchionis.
Fortunata appellatur. Quae nummos modio metitur. Et
modo, modo quid fuit? Ignoscet mihi genius tuus. Nolu-
isses de manu illius panem accipere. Nunc, nec quid
nec quare, in caelum abiit et Trimalchionis topanta est.
"Ad summam, mero meridie si dixerit illi tenebras   37b
esse, credet. Ipse nescit quid habeat, adeo saplutus est.
Sed haec lupatria providet, et ubi non putes. Est tamen

37a

*gustō āre āvī ātus, taste, eat
huc atque illuc, hither and
   thither
Fortunata ae, Lucky Jane — Cp.
   Trimalchio's name, which may
   mean something like High 'n'
   Mighty. His full name is
   Gaius Pompeius Trimalchio
   Maecenatianus. But he especially likes to be called
   Gaius, because this is his
   personal name (given him when
   he became a *libertus)*, and it
   was commonly used, with
   familiar respect, to refer to
   the head of the house, more or
   less as some people say "the
   boss." Cp. Sedgwick's ed.,
   p. 87.
nummos . . . metitur, she counts
   her shekels with a peck
   measure — i.e. like grain.
*īgnōscō ere nōvī nōtus (+ dat.),
   pardon.
*genius ī m, genius — We still
   use the word, but the concept
   has faded. With us a man's
   genius is his special endow-
   ment. With the Romans a man's
   genius (or a woman's *Juno)*
   was a sort of guardian spirit,
   separate from the personality,

so much so that sacrifices
were offered to it, and a man
could even swear by his *genius*
(a woman by her *Juno)*. To
refer to his genius instead of
the man himself was thought to
be a mark of intimate respect,
like "your honor" or "your
highness." Here "Your genius
will pardon me" means something like "I beg your humble
pardon, sir" or "Don't be
offended at what I am going to
say."
*pānis is m, bread, loaf, piece of
   bread
nec quid nec quare, without why
   or wherefore, rhyme or reason
*caelum ī n, the sky, the heav-
   ens, heaven — Fortunata, of
   course, is not dead! "To get
   to heaven" for pagan Romans
   was not to die but to reach the
   height of fortune.
topanta, whole world, all in all

37b

mero meridie, at high noon
tenebras esse, that it is night-
   time
saplutus, wealthy
lupatria (nom.), foxy female

53

malae linguae, pica pulvinaris. Quem amat, amat.
Quem non amat, non amat.

"Ipse Trimalchio fundos habet, qua milvi volant — 37c
nummorum nummos. Argentum in ostiarii illius cella plus
jacet quam quisquam in fortunis habet. Familia vero, babae, babae! Non mehercules puto decimam partem esse
quae dominum suum noverit.

---

*lingua ae f, tongue, language,
   lingo
pica pulvinaris, and she hen-
   pecks him even in bed — Lit. a
   pillow magpie.

37c

fundos, qua . . . nummos, estates
   all over the map — money to

burn! — Lit. farms as far as
kites fly, money of moneys.
*volō āre āvī, fly
in . . . cella, in that butler's
   pantry over there
*jaceō ēre uī, lie
Familia . . . babae, As for
   slaves, well, blow me down —
   See on *familia*, 31b.
*meherculēs, by Hercules, by —

Written Exercise 36, 37

1 *Genius* cannot be translated *(trānsferō)* into our language.
2 They think that birds *(avis is* f.) of this sort can fly right up
   (ūsque) to heaven.
3 Excuse me; I did not notice that you were coming through this
   door.
4 By golly, I have never tasted that kind of fish.
5 The guests received this course with such *(tantus)* applause that
   the whole dining room shook *(intremō ere)*.
6 They knew why the bread was lying on the table.
7 He was so tired *(fessus)* that he did not wish *(nōlō)* to carve the
   fish.

"Noli putare illum quicquam emere. Omnia domi   38a
nascuntur: lana, credrae, piper. Lacte gallinaceum si

38a

domi, on his own estates
credrae, piper, citrons and
   pepper

Lacte gallinaceum, hen's milk —
i.e. anything rare. The expression is as vulgar as the
forms *credrae* and *lacte* for
cedrae and *lac*.

---

quaesieris, invenies. Ad summam, parum illi bona lana
nascebatur; arietes a Tarento emit, et eos culavit in
gregem. Mel Atticum ut domi nasceretur, apes ab
Athenis jussit afferri.

"Ecce intra hos dies scripsit ut illi ex India semen   38b
boletorum mitteretur. Vides tot culcitras? Nulla est
quae non aut conchyliatum aut coccineum tomentum habet.
Tanta est animi beatitudo.

"Reliquos autem collibertos ejus noli contemnere.   38c
Valde sucossi sunt. Vides illum qui in imo imus discumbit? Hodie sua octingenta possidet. De nihilo crevit.
Modo solebat collo suo ligna portare. Ego nemini invideo
si quid deus dedit. Sed non vult sibi male. Itaque pro-

---

parum illi bona, not good enough
   to suit him
arietes a Tarento, rams from
   Tarentum — Where the finest
   sheep were bred.
et . . . gregem, and turned 'em
   loose on his ewes — *Culavit* is
   obscene.
Mel Atticum, Attic honey — The
   best honey in the world came
   from Mt. Hymettus near Athens,
   in Attica.
apes (acc.), bees

38b

*ecce, lo and behold, look, see,
   see here now!
intra hos dies, within the last
   few days
semen (nom.) boletorum, mush-
   room spawn
culcitras (acc.), cushions
aut . . . tomentum, purple or
   scarlet stuffing
beatitudo (nom.), blessedness

38c

*collibertus ī m, fellow freedman
   — See page 2.
contemno ere, look down on
sucossi, wealthy — Lit. juicy
in imo imus, at the foot of the
   table
octingenta, eight hundred
   thousand sesterces — octingenta is a standard abbrevia-
   tion for octingenta deciens —
   milia sestertium (80 × 10,000
   sesterces)
*possideō ēre sēdī sessus,
   possess
*crēscō ere crēvī crētus, grow,
   grow up, swell, grow rich
*soleō ēre — solitus, be accus-
   tomed
*collum ī n, neck
ligna (acc.), firewood — Carrying
   firewood was a menial job.
invideo (+ dat.), envy
Sed . . . male, he puts on airs —
   Literally?

xime casam suam hoc titulo proscripsit: 'C. Pompeius
Diogenes ex kalendis Juliis cenaculum locat; ipse enim
domum emit.'"

(39)
40a

Interim advenerunt pueri ac toralia praeposuerunt
toris in quibus retia erant picta subsessoresque cum
venabulis et totus venationis apparatus. Nondum sciebamus quo mitteremus suspiciones nostras, cum extra triclinium clamor sublatus est ingens, et ecce canes magni
etiam circa mensam discurrere coeperunt. Secutum est hos
repositorium in quo positus erat primae magnitudinis aper,
et quidem pilleatus, e cujus dentibus sportellae dependebant duae, altera caryotis altera thebaicis repleta.

Ceterum ad scindendum aprum non ille Carpus accessit 40b
qui altilia laceraverat, sed barbatus ingens, alicula
subornatus polymita, strictoque venatorio cultro, latus
apri vehementer percussit; statim e vulnere longo turdi

---

casam (acc.), place, shack
titulo (abl.), placard
ex . . . locat, will rent this
  tenement as of July 1st

sportellae (nom.), marketing
  baskets
caryota ae f, walnut date
thebaica ae f, Theban date

40a

toralia praeposuerunt, spread
  couch valances along
*torus ī m, couch, dining couch
retia (nom.), hunting nets
subsessoresque . . . venabulis,
  men lying in wait with hunting
  spears
venatio onis f, hunting, the hunt
*aper apri m, wild boar — The
  ancients' favorite big game.
pilleatus, with a cap of freedom
  on its head — The *pilleus* was
  a cap worn by freed slaves as
  a sign of their new liberty.

40b

scindo ere, carve
altilia (acc.), chickens — See
  36a.
barbatus . . . polymita, a huge,
  bearded man, all decked out
  with a spangled hunting
  jacket
*stringō ere nxī ctus, draw, unsheathe
venatorio cultro (abl.), a hunting
  knife
*percutiō ere cussī cussus,
  strike, knock at
turdus ī m, a thrush

evolaverunt. Parati aucupes cum harundinibus fuerunt et
eos circa triclinium volantes momento temporis exceperunt.

    Inde cum suum turdum cuique jussisset referri Trimal-   40c
chio, adjecit: "Etiam videte quam porcus ille silvaticus
lautam comederit glandem." Statim pueri ad sportellas
accesserunt, quae pendebant e dentibus, thebaicasque et
caryotas ad numerum divisere cenantibus.

---

*ēvolō āre āvī ātus (ē + *volō),
    fly out
aucupes cum harundinibus,
    fowlers with bird snares – The
    snares were made of twigs
    smeared with birdlime, in
    which the birds' feet got stuck
    when they lighted on them. So
    the hunting party is not a boar
    hunt after all, but a bird hunt,
    and besides a serving of roast
    boar each guest will get a
    thrush as a present!

40c

*porcus ī m, pig
*comedō ere ēdī ēsus, eat, eat up
glandem (acc.), (kind of) acorn –
    Boars fed on acorns, but
    Trimalchio refers to the
    baskets of figs, as if, to get
    its food, "this little pig went
    to market!" He's as clever as
    a nursery rhyme!
ad numerum, equally – The guests
    are treated like children at a
    birthday party!

Written Exercise 38-40

1 Do you think that these birds (avis is f.) can fly away?
2 We are accustomed to eat bread and pork, but do not suppose that
  we are accustomed to eat wild boar.
3 Today my fellow freedmen possess all their rights (jūs jūris n.). –
  See p. 58.
4 See, this pig has grown big.
5 We have tables and trays, but we are not accustomed to have
  dining couches.
6 With drawn sword the priest (sacerdōs ōtis) will strike the neck of
  the pig.

    Interim ego, qui privatum habebam secessum, in multas 41a
cogitationes deductus sum, quare aper pilleatus intrasset.
Postquam itaque omnes bacalusias consumpsi, coepi

41a

secessum (acc.), meditation

pilleatus, wearing a liberty cap
bacalusias (acc.), improbable
    speculations

interrogare illum interpretem meum quod me torqueret. At
ille: "Plane etiam hoc servus tuus indicare potest. Non
enim aenigma est, sed res aperta. Hic aper, cum heri
summa cena eum vindicasset, a convivis dimissus est.
Itaque hodie tamquam libertus in triclinium revertitur."
Damnavi ego stuporem meum et nihil amplius interrogavi,
ne viderer numquam inter honestos cenasse.

Dum haec loquimur, puer pulcherrimus vitibus he-   41b
derisque redimitus, modo Bromium, interdum Lyaeum,
Euhiumque confessus, uvas circumtulit et poemata domini
sui altissima voce recitavit. Ad quem sonum conversus
Trimalchio, "Dionyse," inquit, "Liber esto!"

---

quod me torqueret, the question
  that was torturing my mind
*plānē, clearly, obviously,
  utterly
servus tuus, your humble servant
  − i.e. the speaker − "I".
cum heri . . . vindicasset, when
  the main course of yesterday's
  dinner claimed a legal right to
  him − Legal language and
  personification, implying that
  the dinner had gone to court to
  claim the boar as its own
  property, as if the boar were
  a runaway slave.
dimissus est, was dismissed − By
  not eating him, the guests had
  pronounced judgment, and dismissed the case, thus giving the
  boar his "freedom" − hence the
  liberty cap!
*lībertus ī m, a freedman − See
  page 37.
Damnavi . . . meum, I too pronounced judgment, condemning
  my own stupidity. − Note the
  ironical satire of this passage.
  It is not Encolpius who is stupid, but the freedmen. Petronius
  represents them as so con-
  scious of their successful
  "social mobility" that even

their amusements take ex-
travagantly silly forms incom-
prehensible to other people.

41b

vitibus . . . confessus, garlanded
with vine leaves and ivy, im-
personating (Dionysus, the
Greek god of wine) as Roaring,
then Relaxing, and again
Reveling
uvas (acc.), grapes
*sonus ī m, sound, noise
Liber esto: As it stands in the
text, Liber esto means "Be
Liber," i.e. "Now that you
have shown us various Greek
forms of Dionysus, show us
also the Roman form," as if
Liber, the Roman name of
Dionysus, were an epithet like
Bromius, etc. above. But
Liber esto sounds the same as
liber esto, "Be free," the
legal formula used in freeing
slaves. The slave boy pretends to understand the words
in the latter sense, and at
once seizes the chance to
claim his freedom.

Puer detraxit pilleum apro capitique suo imposuit.   41c
Tum Trimalchio rursus adjecit: "Non negabitis me,"
inquit, "habere liberum patrem." Laudavimus dictum
Trimalchionis, et circumeuntem puerum sane perbasiamus.

Ab hoc ferculo Trimalchio ad lasanum surrexit. Nos   41d
libertatem sine tyranno nacti coepimus invitare conviva-
rum sermones. Dama itaque primus, "Dies," inquit,
"nihil est. Dum versas te, nox fit. Itaque nihil est
melius quam de cubiculo recta in triclinium ire.

"Et mundum frigus habuimus. Vix me balneus   41e
calfecit. Tamen potio vestiarius est; staminatas duxi
et plane matus sum. Vinus mihi in cerebrum abiit."

Excepit Seleucus fabulae partem et "Ego," inquit,   42a

41c

pilleum (acc.), the liberty cap
liberum patrem – A still more
  ridiculous application of the
  same pun. Trimalchio can
  claim to have a "freeborn
  father" (and therefore never to
  have been a slave at all), because he has a slave who im-
  personates Dionysus, who was
  frequently called Father Liber
  (*Pater Liber*). Thus the slave
  boy must remain a slave to per-
  form a function that gives his
  master freeborn status!
*sāne, really, indeed
*(per)bāsiō āre āvī ātus, kiss
  (soundly)

41d

ad lasanum, to use the bathroom
*surgō ere surrēxī, rise up, get
  up (from table)
tyranno (abl.), tyrant – i.e.
  Trimalchio. In his absence the
  guests *(nos)*, in contrast to the
  slave boy, had gained freedom.

*sermō ōnis m, conversation, talk
Dama – Name of one of the *convivae.*
Dum . . . te, before you can get
  anything done
de cubiculo, from your bedroom
recta, straight – Dama seems to
  mean: You can't achieve anything anyway. Better just
  sleep and eat.

41e

mundum frigus (acc.), right crisp
  weather
balneus = balneum – Dama mixes
  drinks, and genders too!
calfecit, warmed up
vestiarius, as good as an *over*-
  coat
staminatas duxi, I've had an
  *over*dose
matus (nom.), soused
vinus = vinum – He's mixed up
  again.
cerebrum (acc.), brain, head

42a

*fābula ae f, talk, story

"non cotidie lavor. Baliscus enim fullo est, et aqua dentes habet. Nec sane lavare potui; fui enim hodie in funus. Homo bellus, tam bonus Chrysanthus animam ebulliit. Modo, modo me appellavit. Videor mihi cum illo loqui. Heu, eheu! Utres inflati ambulamus. Minoris quam muscae sumus. Muscae tamen aliquam virtutem habent; nos non pluris sumus quam bullae.

"Et quid si non abstinax fuisset? Quinque dies   42b
aquam in os suum non conjecit, non micam panis. Tamen abiit ad plures. Medici illum perdiderunt, immo magis malus fatus. Medicus enim nihil aliud est quam animi consolatio.

"Tamen bene elatus est, vitali lecto, stragulis bonis.   42c
Ploratus est optime (manu misit aliquot) etiam si maligne illum ploravit uxor. Quid si non illam optime accepisset? Sed mulier quae mulier milvinum genus. Neminem nihil boni facere oportet; aeque est enim ac si in puteum conjicias. Sed antiquus amor cancer est."

Baliscus . . . est, I'd just as soon get myself dry-cleaned as take a bath

funus (acc.), funeral

*bellus a um, nice, pretty

Chrysanthus . . . ebulliit, Mr. Goldflower blew his last bubble of breath

Utres inflati, mere bags of wind

*ambulō āre āvī ātus, walk (around)

muscae (nom.), flies

bullae (nom.), bubbles

42b

abstinax (nom.), a faster — i.e. one who fasts; both words, English and Latin, coined for effect.

*ōs ōris, n, mouth

micam (acc.), crumb

plures, the place where most folks are

*medicus ī m, doctor

*immō, rather, on the contrary, furthermore, in fact

fatus = fatum ī n, fate, luck — Like Dama, Seleucus is shaky on genders.

42c

bene elatus . . . bonis, he had a swell funeral, with a real bier and a fine pall

*plōrō āre āvī ātus, mourn, weep for

*manū mīsit, he manumitted — A term regularly used of freeing slaves. Goldflower had apparently freed some slaves in his will, to ensure having some grateful mourners.

maligne, grudgingly

accepisset, he had treated

milvinum genus, is kin to the vulture

aeque . . . conjicias, (being good to a woman) is just like throwing something down a well

cancer, a crab, a thing that grips you

60

1 On the contrary, I do not think that a freedman is of more (account) than a slave.
2 Obviously, the conversation of these freedmen is nothing but (other than) silly *(merus a um)* stories.
3 Do not suppose that that man is really of less (consequence) than you (are).
4 Don't weep; I will manumit these boys.
5 On the contrary, the doctor went out to (take a) walk in the woods.
6 You will not deny that this fish has a large mouth.
7 The sailor really kissed all the pretty girls.
8 (When) this sound (was) heard, they got up (from the table).
9 Have you not learned to say in Latin *(Latīnē)* "to go, I am going, I shall go, I have gone, you (singular) are going away, he is going out, we are going around, you (plural) are going across, they are going back"?

Molestus fuit, Philerosque proclamavit: "Vivorum   43a
meminerimus. Ille habet quod sibi debebatur: honeste
vixit, honeste obiit. Quid habet quod queratur? Ab asse
crevit, et paratus fuit quadrantem de stercore dentibus
tollere. Itaque crevit, quicquid crevit, tamquam favus.
Puto mehercules illum reliquisse solida centum, et omnia
in nummis habuit. De re tamen ego verum dicam, qui
linguam caninam comedi: durae buccae fuit, linguosus –
discordia, non homo.

"Frater ejus fortis fuit, amicus amico, manu plena,   43b

43a

*meminī isse (+ gen.), remember – "Let's remember the living" is proverbial for "Let's talk about something cheerful."
*honestē (cp. *honestus*), respectably
obiit, he died
*ās assis m, an as (a coin of small value), penny
quadrantem de stercore, a dime from a dunghill

favus, a honeycomb
solida centum, a cool hundred thousand sesterces
nummis (abl.), hard cash
caninam = canis (gen.) – This proverb seems to refer to the Cynic (i.e. Doglike) philosophers, who would tell the truth at any cost.
durae buccae, loud-mouthed
linguosus, a big blather – Literally?

uncta mensa. Et inter initia malam parram pilavit, sed recorrexit costas illius prima vindemia; vendidit enim vinum quanti ipse voluit. Et quod illius mentum sustulit, hereditatem accepit, ex qua plus involavit quam illi relictum est. Plane Fortunae filius, in manu illius plumbum aurum fiebat."

Haec Phileros dixit, illa Ganymedes: "Narratis quod   44a
nec ad caelum nec ad terram pertinet, cum interim nemo
curat quid annona mordet. Non mehercules hodie buccam
panis invenire potui. Et quomodo siccitas perseverat!
Jam annum esuritio fuit. Aediles? Male eis eveniat, qui
cum pistoribus colludunt 'Serva me, servabo te.' Itaque
populus minutus laborat, nam isti majores maxillae semper Saturnalia agunt.
   "O si haberemus illos leones, quos ego hic inveni   44b
cum primum ex Asia veni! Illud erat vivere. Memini
Safinium. Tunc habitabat ad Arcum Veterem, me puero —
piper, non homo. Is quacumque ibat, terram adurebat. Sed

43b

uncta (abl.), lavish
malam . . . pilavit, he plucked an
  ill-omened owl — This seems
  to mean that he had hard luck.
sed . . . vindemia, but his first
  crop of grapes mended his ribs
  — i.e. got him on his feet again.
*vēndō ere didī, sell
mentum (acc.), chin — "To lift a
  man's chin" is a proverbial
  way of saying "to give him a
  boost."
hereditatem (acc.), an inheritance
involavit, he pounced upon —
  Literally?
plumbum (nom.), lead
*aurum ī n, gold

44a

quid . . . mordet, how the cost of
  food gnaws on us

buccam (acc.), mouthful
*quōmodo, how, as
siccitas perseverat, the drought
  continues
esuritio (nom.), scarcity of food
Aediles . . . colludunt, Commissioners? Damn them! They're
  in cahoots with the bakeries. —
  Aediles were public officials
  in charge of the food supply;
  by creating shortages, they
  could run prices up.
minutus (nom.), little
isti . . . maxillae, the upper
  crust, the big shots
Saturnalia — Midwinter festival,
  lavish as New Year's Eve

44b

leones (acc.), lions; heroes
ad . . . Veterem, near Old Arch
piper, pepper; a firebrand
quacumque, wherever
adurebat, he scorched

rectus, sed certus, amicus amico, cum quo audacter posses
in tenebris micare.

"In curia autem quomodo singulos pilabat! Sic illius   44c
vox crescebat tamquam tuba. Sed in foro vel in via quam
benignus resalutare, nomina omnium reddere, tamquam
unus de nobis! Itaque illo tempore annona pro luto erat.
Asse panem quem emisses non potuisses cum altero
comedere. Nunc oculum bublum vidi majorem.

"Heu, heu! Cotidie pejus. Haec colonia retroversus   44d
crescit tamquam coda vituli. Sed quare nos habemus
aedilem trium cauniarum, qui sibi mavult assem quam
vitam nostram? Itaque domi gaudet. Plus in die
nummorum accipit quam alter patrimonium habet. Jam
scio unde acceperit denarios mille aureos. Sed si nos
coleos haberemus, non tantum sibi placeret. Nunc
populus est domi leones, foras vulpes.

"Quod ad me attinet, jam pannos meos comedi;   44e
brevi tempore casulas meas vendam. Quid enim futurum

---

rectus, straightforward, honest
in tenebris micare, match pen-
　nies in the dark — See on
　Bucca, 64d

44c

curia (abl.), the senate-house
pilabat, he used to snatch 'em
　baldheaded
quam . . . reddere, how kind he
　was to answer when you spoke
　to him, calling everyone by
　name — Discuss these words
　in class.
annona . . . erat, groceries were
　dirtcheap
bublum, of an ox or a cow —
　Loaves of bread were round,
　like buns.

44d

*colōnia ae f, town

retroversus, backwards
coda vituli, a calf's tail
aedilem . . . cauniarum, a com-
　missioner who's not worth a
　fig
gaudet, gloats
nummorum (with *plus*), cash
*patrimonium ī n, patrimony,
　estate
coleos (acc.), any guts — The
　Latin word is even more vulgar.
foras vulpes, foxes outside —
　People talk big in private but
　keep a poker face in public.

44e

Quod . . . attinet, As for my own
　case
pannos meos, my duds, the shirt
　off my back — He has sold
　clothes to buy food.
casulas (acc.), li'l ole home-
　stead

est, si nec dei nec homines hujus coloniae miserentur?
Ego puto omnia illa a deis fieri. Nemo enim caelum caelum
putat, nemo jejunium servat, nemo Jovem pili facit, sed
omnes opertis oculis bona sua computant.

"Antea stolatae ibant nudis pedibus in Clivum,   44f
mentibus puris, et Jovem aquam exorabant. Itaque statim
urceatim plovebat, aut tunc aut numquam, et omnes redi-
bant udi tamquam mures. Itaque dei pedes lanatos habent
quia nos religiosi non sumus. Agri jacent –"
"Oro te," inquit Echion centonarius, "melius   45a
loquere. Non mehercules patria melior dici potest – si
homines haberet. Sed laborat hoc tempore, nec haec sola.
Tu si aliubi fueris, dices hic porcos coctos ambulare.
Et ecce habituri sumus munus excellente in triduo –
familia non lanisticia, sed plurimi liberti. Et Titus

---

miserentur (+ gen.), take pity on
jejunium (acc.), a fast
pili facit, gives a darn for – Lit.
  regards him as worth a hair
  (gen.).
opertis (with *oculis*), shut, i.e.
  selfish

44f

stolatae (nom.), matrons in their
  best robes
in Clivum, up the Hill – To the
  temple of Jupiter, god of rain.
urceatim plovebat, it rained
  bucketfuls – Lit. in pitcherfuls
udi (nom.), wet
*mūs mūris m or f, mouse –
  Ganymedes seems to be thinking of drowned mice.
lanatos (acc.), wrapped in wool –
  To creep up on men unawares
  (?).
*quia, because

45a

centonarius (nom.), the ragman
melius, better – i.e. not so
  gloomily
si, if (it) just . . .
aliubi, somewhere else
coctos (acc.), roast(ed)
munus excellente (acc.), a
  tremenjious exhibition (of
  gladiators) – Echion says
  excellente for *excellens.*
familia . . . liberti, not just a
  troupe of regulars but mostly
  veterans – Gladiators were re-
  quired to live in barracks,
  supervised by a trainer *(la-
  nista)* for a given time. Even
  after discharge from the regu-
  lar troupe *(familia lanisticia),*
  some would fight voluntarily.
  These were called *liberti* because they had served their
  time. Such *liberti*, being most
  skillful, would put on a
  "tremenjious" show.
Titus – Name of the magistrate
  who is backing the show.

noster magnum animum habet et est caldicerebrius. Aut
hoc aut illud erit, quid utique. Nam illi amicus sum.

"Non est miscix. Ferrum optimum daturus est, sine   45b
fuga, carnarium in medio, ut amphitheater videat. Et
habet unde; non sentiet patrimonium illius, et sempiterno
nominabitur. Jam Manios aliquot habet et mulierem
essedariam et servum Glyconis, qui deprehensus est, cum
dominam suam delectaretur. Videbis populi rixam inter
zelotypos et amasiunculos.

"Glyco autem servum ad bestias dedit. Hoc est se   45c
ipsum traducere. Quid servus peccavit, qui coactus est
facere? Magis illa matella digna fuit quam taurus jactaret.
Quid autem Glyco putabat Hermogenis filiam umquam
bonum exitum facturam? Ille milvo volanti poterat ungues
resecare; colubra restem non parit. Glyco, Glyco dedit
suas. Itaque quamdiu vixerit, habebit stigmam, nec illam
nisi Orcus delebit. Sed sibi quisque peccat.

---

caldicerebrius, hot-brained,
  original
quid, something (real)
*utique, anyhow, especially

45b

miscix, a mixer-upper, bungler
carnarium, butchery
unde, the where-from — i.e. the
  money to do it with
nominabitur, he will be famous —
  Literally?
Manios (acc.), clowns
essedariam (acc.), charioteer
Glyconis, of Glyco's
deprehensus est, was caught
*domina ae f, mistress (Cp.
  *dominus)
*dēlectō āre āvī ātus, delight —
  Echion makes this verb deponent. Don't follow his
  example.
populi . . . amasiunculos, you'll
  see rivalry a-plenty among the
  fans, Othellos versus Gigolos

—The latter rooting for the
  slave.

45c

traducere, to disgrace
pecco are, do wrong
matella (nom.), slut — Lit. pot; he
  means Glyco's wife, the real
  culprit.
quam . . . jactaret, for a bull to
  toss around
Ille milvo . . . parit, He (Hermogenes, father of Glyco's wife)
  could cut the claws of a kite
  on the wing, and a viper does
  not beget a (harmless) rope —
  i.e. Hermogenes' daughter is
  as tricky as he was.
dedit suas, has made a mess of
  his life (?) — There is no satis-
  factory explanation of this
  idiom.
stigmam (acc.), disgrace
peccat, makes mistakes

1 I think he's a mouse, not a man.
2 By golly, this boy is growing like a pig.
3 The boys were as quiet (silent) as mice.
4 It's difficult to live respectably in this town.
5 How he ought *(dēbeō)* to remember his mistress!
6 O, if I (only) had such *(tantus a um)* an estate!
7 If I had lots of (much) gold, I would live better.
8 If his master were here *(adsum)*, he would not be selling wine for a penny.
9 If your father were alive, you would not do that.
10 I believe that all these things happen because men do not care *(faciō)* a darn *(pīlī)* for the gods.
11 These things would happen anyhow.
12 He is going to receive a large patrimony.
13 They were going to give the wine to their master.
14 This wine is going to delight our master.
15 We were going to send this gold to our friends.

"Videris mihi, Agamemnon, dicere: 'Quid iste argutat 46a
molestus?' Quia tu, qui potes loquere, non loquis. Non
es unus de nobis, et ideo pauperorum verba derides.
Scimus te prae litteras fatuum esse. Quid ergo est?
Aliqua die te persuadeam ut ad villam venias et videas
casulas nostras? Inveniemus quod manducemus. Belle
erit etiam si omnia hoc anno tempestas dispare pallavit.
Inveniemus ergo unde saturi fiamus.

46a

argutat (= argutatur), does . . .
  keep ranting away
loquere = loqui; loquis =
  loqueris — Echion needs to
  review his deponents. Do
  you?
*ideō, for that reason, that's the
  reason why
*pauper eris, a poor man — Third
  declension, but Echion makes
  it second.

*dērīdeō ēre sī sus (dē + *rīdeō),
  laugh at, have the laugh on
  (someone)
fatuum, just crazy
casulas nostras, my little farm
quod manducemus, something to
  nibble on
*bellē, nice, nicely, neatly
dispare pallavit, made everything
  (omnia) sprout unevenly
saturi (nom.), full (of food)

"Et jam tibi discipulus crescit cicaro meus. Jam   46b
quattuor partes dicit. Si vixerit, habebis ad latus ser-
vulum. Nam quicquid temporis illi vacat, caput de tabula
non tollit. Ingeniosus est, etiam si in aves morbosus
est. Ego illi jam tres cardeles occidi, et dixi quod
mustella comedit. Invenit tamen alias nenias, et
libentissime pingit.

"Ceterum jam Graeculis calcem impingit et Latinas   46c
coepit non male appetere. Emi ergo nunc puero aliquot
libra rubricata, quia volo illum ad domusionem aliquid
de jure gustare. Habet haec res panem. Nam litteris
satis inquinatus est.

"Quod si resilierit, destinavi illum aliquid artificii   46d
docere, aut tonstreinum aut praeconem aut certe causidicum,
quod illi auferre nil possit nisi Orcus. Ideo illi cotidie
clamo: 'Primigeni, crede mihi, quicquid discis, tibi

46b

discipulus, (to be) a pupil
cicaro (nom.), little lad
partes, fractiones — He can di-
    vide by four.
vacat, is free, available
tabula (abl.), writing-tablet
ingeniosus (nom.), smart
in aves morbosus, crazy about
    birds
cardeles (acc.), goldfinches
quod, that — In vulgar and late
    Latin *quod* introduces indirect
    statements.
mustella, weasel
nenias (acc.), hobbies

46c

Graeculis (litteris) . . . impingit,
    he's getting a foothold in
    Greek
libra rubricata, law books —
    Echion gives *liber* the wrong
    gender. What should he have
    said?

ad domusionem, for practical use
satis inquinatus, pretty well
    greased up — *Litterae* com-
    prised literature, history,
    philosophy, rhetoric, social
    studies, etc., the liberal edu-
    cation of the upper classes.
    Echion thinks his boy's work
    in college prep. subjects has
    put him well on the way
    toward higher education.

46d

*quod sī, but if, and if
resilierit, he shies away from it
destinavi, I am determined
*artificium ī n, trade, profession
aut tonstreinum . . . causidicum,
    either barbering, or an
    auctioneer, or if need be, an
    attorney
Primigeni (voc.), Firstborn —
    Ironical name for an only
    child! Note the jingle of
    sound in *Prímigeni, créde mihi.*

discis. Vides Phileronem causidicum. Si non didicisset,
hodie famem a labris non abigeret. Modo, modo collo suo
circumferebat onera venalia. Nunc etiam adversus Norbanum se extendit. Litterae thesaurum est, et artificium
numquam moritur.' ' '

Ejusmodi fabulae vibrabant, cum Trimalchio intravit,   47a
et tersa fronte, unguento manus lavit. Nec adhuc sciebamus nos in medio lautitiarum, quod ajunt, clivo laborare.
Nam cum mundatis ad symphoniam mensis, tres albi porci
in triclinium adducti sunt, quorum unum Bimum nomenclator esse dicebat, alterum Trimum, tertium vero jam
Sexennem, ego putabam petauristarios intrasse et porcos,
sicut in circulis mos est, portenta aliqua facturos.

Sed Trimalchio, exspectatione discussa, "Quem,"   47b
inquit, "ex eis vultis in cenam statim fieri? Gallum enim
gallinaceum, penthiacum, et ejusmodi nenias rustici
faciunt; mei coci etiam vitulos aeno coctos solent facere."

---

*labrum ī n, lip
venalia (with *onera*), of things to
    sell — Cp. *vēndō*.
Norbanum (acc.) — A prominent
    politician
Litterae . . . est, eddication are
    a treasure — Bad English for
    bad Latin. Given *thēsaurus* ī
    m, how would you correct
    Echion's sentence?
*morior ī mortuus, moritūrus, die

Such slaves were called
    nomenclatores, name-callers.
In Trimalchio's house even the
    pigs have their *nomenclator!*
Trimum (acc.), Mr. Threeyearsold
Sexennem (acc.), Mr. Sixyearsold
petauristarios (acc.), circus per-
    formers
in circulis, with people cluster-
    ing round them in the street
portenta (acc.), remarkable tricks

47a

vibrabant, were (was) in the air
quod, as — Literally?
in medio clivo, only half way up
    the hill
mundatis (abl.), cleared
Bimum (acc.), Mr. Twoyearsold
nomenclator, the announcer — Men
    of affairs had slaves in attend-
    ance whose duty it was to re-
    mind them of the names of
    people they happened to meet.

47b

discussa (abl.), being shattered
Gallum . . . facere, For even
    country people make fried
    chicken, hash, and that sort of
    stuff, but my chefs regularly
    cook even whole calves in one
    pot — Of the words in this sen-
    tence you have seen more than
    half before. How many can
    you spot?

Continuoque cocum vocari jussit, et non exspectata   47c
electione nostra, maximum natu jussit occidi, et clara
voce: "Ex quota decuria es?" Cum ille se ex quadragesima
esse respondisset, "Empticius an," inquit, "domi natus?"
"Neutrum," inquit cocus, "sed testamento Pansae tibi
relictus sum."
   "Vide ergo," ait, "ut diligenter ponas; si non, te   47d
jubebo in decuriam viatorum conjici." Et cocum quidem
potentiae admonitum in culinam obsonium duxit.
   Trimalchio autem miti ad nos vultu respexit et   48a
"Vinum," inquit, "si non placet, mutabo. Vos illud
oportet bonum faciatis. Deorum beneficio non emo, sed
nunc quicquid ad salivam facit, in suburbano nascitur eo,
quod ego adhuc non novi. Dicitur confine esse
Tarraciniensibus et Tarentinis. Nunc conjungere agellis

47c

*cocus ī m, a cook
electione (abl.), choice
maximum natu, the oldest one
Ex quota . . . es, What's your
   squad number? – The slaves
   are organized like an army!
Empticius, Were you acquired by
   purchase?
testamento Pansae, in Pansa's
   will

47d

ponas, you serve (the pig)
decuriam viatorum, the courier
   squad – The ancient equiva-
   lent of the telephone.
potentiae, of (his master's)
   power
culinam (acc.), kitchen
obsonium (nom.), the groceries –
   i.e. *illi tres albi porci.*
   Doubtless they were straining
   on their leashes.

48a

miti (abl.), kindly
(ut) faciatis, (that) you should
   regard . . . as – The wine
   already served *(illud)* is his
   own vintage and it *must* be
   good.
ad salivam facit, makes your
   mouth water
suburbano (abl. neut.), a sub-
   urban estate of mine
confine . . . Tarentinis, close to
   the Tarracinians and the
   Tarentines – Pompous, alliter-
   ative reference to two far-
   separated towns in Italy, show-
   ing ignorance of both geography
   and word-formation. Imagine
   someone's claiming to own a
   place close to New Yorkers
   and "New Orleansers."
agellis (dat.), my odds and ends
   of farms – *Agellus*, diminutive
   of *ager*, here suggests mock
   modesty.

69

Siciliam volo, ut cum Africam libuerit ire, per meos fines navigem.

"Sed narra tu mihi, Agamemnon, quam controversiam   48b
hodie declamasti? Ego etiam si orator non sum, in
domusionem tamen litteras didici. Et ne me putes studia
fastiditum, tres bybliothecas habeo, unam Graecam,
alteram Latinam. Dic ergo, si me amas, aliquid
declamationis tuae."

Cum dixisset Agamemnon, "Pauper et dives inimici   48c
erant," ait Trimalchio, "Quid est pauper?" "Urbane,"
inquit Agamemnon, et aliquam controversiam exposuit.
Statim Trimalchio, "Hoc," inquit, "si factum est, controversia non est; si factum non est, nihil est."

Haec aliaque cum maximis prosequeremur lauda-   48d
tionibus, "Rogo," inquit, "Agamemnon mihi carissime,
numquid duodecim aerumnas Herculis tenes, aut de Ulixe

Siciliam (acc.) — The large island at the toe of Italy

Africam (acc.) — He thinks of Africa as a city or small island. How does his language show this?

libuerit, when I take the notion

fines — This word implies dry land!

48b

controversiam (acc.), disputation — A kind of oratory which Agamemnon, as a professor of rhetoric, would practise.

in domusionem, well enough for practical purposes

me fastiditum (esse), that I'se been despiseful about — Bad English, bad Latin. Trimalchio makes *fastidire,* which sounds more or less pompous in any case, into a deponent.

bybliothecas, liberies (libraries) — Trimalchio mispronounces

bibliothecas, probably to show that he knows it is Greek.

48c

dives (nom.), a rich man

Urbane, Clever! — Trimalchio thinks himself cute when he pretends not to know what a poor man is. Agamemnon is too courteous to disillusion him.

Statim Trimalchio, etc. — Beware of the old punster! *Controversia* = disputation = a dispute: *factum est* = it is over with = it took place.

48d

numquid (in memoria) tenes, I don't 'spose you remember, do you?

aerumnas (acc.) Herculis, miseries of Hercules

Ulixe (abl.), Ulysses

fabulam, quemadmodum illi Cyclops pollicem porcino extorsit? Solebam haec ego puer apud Homerum legere.

"Nam Sibyllam quidem Cumis ego ipse oculis meis   48e
vidi in ampulla pendere, et cum illi pueri dicerent,
'Sibylla, ti theleis?' respondebat illa, 'Apothanein
thelo.' "

Nondum haec efflaverat omnia, cum repositorium cum   49a
porco ingenti mensam occupavit. Mirari nos celeritatem
coepimus et jurare ne gallum quidem gallinaceum tam
cito percoqui potuisse, tanto quidem magis quod longe
major nobis porcus videbatur esse quam paulo ante aper
fuerat. Deinde magis magisque Trimalchio intuens eum,
"Quid? Quid?" inquit, "porcus hic non est exinteratus?
Non mehercules est. Voca, voca cocum in medio."

Cum constitisset ad mensam cocus tristis et diceret   49b
se oblitum esse exinterare, "Quid? Oblitus?"
Trimalchio exclamat, "Putes illum piper et cuminum non

---

illi . . . extorsit, the Cyclops
  twisted his thumb off after he
  had turned him into a pig
*legō ere lēgī lēctus, read
Homerum (acc.) — Do your impres-
  sions of Homer tally with
  Trimalchio's? If not, why
  not?

48e

Sibylla ae f, a Sibyl — Sibyls
  were prophetic old women, who
  had nothing to do with Homer.
Cumis, at Cumae — The Sibyl of
  Cumae was the best known because of her part in Vergil's
  Aeneid, the action of which
  took place a thousand years
  before Trimalchio was born.
ampulla (abl.), a bottle — The
  Sibyl is so old she has
  shriveled to the size of a
  grasshopper, like Tithonus.
ti theleis, what do you want?
Apothanein thelo, I want to die —

Trimalchio quotes the conversation in Greek to impress
  Agamemnon.

49a

efflaverat, had he wheezed out —
  It seems Trimalchio found the
  Greek words (the th's) hard to
  say.
gallum gallinaceum (acc.), a
  chicken
*cito, quickly
percoqui, (to) be cooked, be done
  — The pig is Mr. Sixyearsold.
intuens (nom.), looking closely
  at
exinteratus — From exinterare, to
  gut, i.e. dress (for cooking)

49b

tristis (nom.), looking glum
piper et cuminum (acc.), pepper
  and cumin — We would say pepper and salt.

71

conjecisse. Despolia!" Non fit mora, despoliatur cocus
atque inter duos tortores maestus consistit. Deprecari
tamen omnes coeperunt et dicere, "Solet fieri. Rogamus
mittas. Postea, si fecerit, nemo nostrum pro illo
rogabit."

Ego, crudelissimae severitatis, non potui me tenere,   49c
sed conversus ad aurem Agamemnonis, "Plane," inquam,
"hic debet esse nequissimus. Aliquis oblivisceretur
porcum exinterare? Non mehercules ignoscerem, si
piscem praeterisset."

At non Trimalchio, qui relaxato in hilaritatem vultu,   49d
"Ergo," inquit, "quia tam malae memoriae es, palam
nobis illum exintera." Recepta cocus tunica cultrum
arripuit porcique ventrem hinc atque illinc timida manu
secuit. Nec mora, ex plagis ponderis inclinatione
crescentibus tomacula cum botulis effusa sunt.

despolia — From *despoliare*, to
   strip (for flogging)
tortores (acc.), floggers
maestus (nom.), woebegone
deprecari, to beg him off
(ut) mittas, that you let him off —
   Note omission of *ut*.

49c

crudelissimae severitatis, (being
   a man) of the most unmerciful
   austerity
nequissimus, utterly good for
   nothing
praeterisset, had merely forgotten
   to clean — Literally?

49d

*hilaritās tātis f, gaiety, fun
palam nobis, right here in front
   of us
cultrum arripuit, snatched up a
   knife
ventrem hinc atque illinc secuit,
   slashed the belly this way and
   that
ex plagis . . . crescentibus, from
   the gashes, which widened with
   the sinking of the mass (behind
   them)
tomacula cum botulis, sausages
   and black puddings
*effundō ere fūdī fūsus, pour out

Written Exercise 46-49

1 That's the reason why I believed that the cook himself was pouring out all the wine, had poured (it) out, (and) was going to
   (continue to) pour (it) out.
2 Obviously he appeared to be a poor (man). For that reason they
   were all laughing at him.
3 By jinks, I would not excuse him (dative), even if he were my
   own son.

4 I do not know why the gaiety so quickly fled *(fugiō)* from his face. See p. 74.
5 We intend (are going) to read a story in Homer. Have you not learned to read?
6 But if I can (will be able to) persuade you to dine at my house, it will be nice.
7 And if his father had taught him a trade, he would not be poor.
8 If the wine did not please his guests (dative), he was going to change it.
9 He has such a poor memory (is of so bad a memory) that he often forgets his own name.
10 He has such a poor memory that he does not remember his best friends.
11 I'll die if your father will not excuse us.
12 They say that a freedman never dies poor.
13 That's why I thought his lips looked white.
14 Do not forget that your son is dead.

Plausum post hoc automatum familia dedit, et "Gaio 50a
feliciter!" conclamavit. Nec non cocus potione honoratus
est et argentea corona, poculumque in lance accepit
Corinthia. Quam cum Agamemnon propius inspiceret, ait
Trimalchio, "Solus sum qui vera Corinthea habeam."
Exspectabam ut pro reliqua insolentia diceret sibi vasa
Corintho afferri.

50a

automatum (acc.), neat surprise
*fēlīciter, fortunately, luckily —
  This adverb is used to express
  good wishes, blessings, etc.,
  sometimes by itself, as
  Feliciter, Good luck! or with a
  dative, *Feliciter tibi,* Best
  wishes to you! Some verb,
  eveniat or *fiat,* is implied.
  Here *Gaio Feliciter* is something like Hurrah for the boss!
  See on *Fortunata,* 37a.
*corōna ae f, crown, garland —
  Worn at parties.
poculum (acc.), goblet
lance Corinthia (abl.), a platter
  of Corinthian bronze — Very
  costly, said to be made of an
  alloy of silver or gold.
propius, quite closely
Corinthea, Corinthian bronze
  ware
insolentia (abl.), arrogance
vasa (acc.) tableware
Corintho, from Corinth — Greek
  city famous for its bronze and
  other ware.

Sed ille melius: "Et forsitan," inquit, "quaeris   50b
quare solus Corinthea vera possideam? Quia scilicet
aerarius a quo emo Corinthus vocatur. Quid est autem
Corintheum, nisi quis Corinthum habet?

"Et ne me putetis nesapium esse, valde bene scio   50c
unde primum Corinthea nata sint. Cum Ilium captum est,
Hannibal, homo vafer et magnus stelio, omnes statuas
aeneas et aureas et argenteas in unum rogum congessit
et eas incendit; factae sunt in unum, aerea miscellanea.
Ita ex hac massa fabri sustulerunt et fecerunt catilla et
paropsides et statuncula. Sic Corinthea nata sunt, ex
omnibus in unum, nec hoc nec illud.

"Ignoscetis mihi quod dixero: ego malo mihi vitrea.
Certe non olunt. Quod si non frangerentur, mallem mihi
quam aurum. Nunc autem vilia sunt.

"Fuit tamen faber qui fecit phialam vitream quae non   51a
frangebatur. Admissus ergo Caesarem est cum suo munere.
Deinde fecit porrigere Caesari et illam in pavimentum
projecit. Caesar non pote valdius quam expavit.

50b

forsitan, perhaps
*scīlicet, of course, naturally
aerarius (nom.), bronze dealer
Quid est . . . habet, Besides,
  what Corinthian (ware) is there,
  unless someone has a
  Corinth(us)? – A wretched pun!

50c

nesapium (acc.), an ignoramus
Ilium (nom.), Troy
Hannibal (nom.) – Carthaginian
  general, who lived a thousand
  years after the fall of Troy.
vafer (nom.), crafty
stelio (nom.), a rogue
aeneas (adj.), bronze
rogum (acc.), funeral pyre – As
  if the statues were human
  bodies being cremated.
Congere ere gessī gestum, col-
  lect, heap up
aerea miscellanea, bronze hash

ex, some of
fabri (nom.), craftsmen
catilla . . . statuncula (acc.),
  bowls, platters, and figurines
olunt, smell – Corinthian bronze
  was supposed to have a
  peculiar odor.
vilia, cheap

51a

faber (nom.), a craftsman
phialam (acc.), cup
Caesarem, to the presence of the
  Emperor – Which emperor this
  was is unknown.
munere (abl.), masterpiece –
  Munus implies a contribution
  to the public good.
fecit porrigere, he made as if to
  hand it
pavimentum (acc.), the floor
Caesar . . . expavit, the Emperor
  couldn't have been more
  startled

"At ille sustulit phialam de terra. Collisa erat tam-   51b
quam vasum aeneum. Deinde martiolum de sinu protulit,
et phialam otio belle correxit.

"Hoc facto, putabat se solium Jovis tenere, utique   51c
postquam Caesar illi dixit, 'Numquid alius scit hanc
condituram vitreorum?' Vide modo. Postquam negavit,
jussit illum Caesar decollari, quia enim, si scitum esset,
aurum pro luto haberemus.

"In argento plane studiosus sum. Habeo scyphos   52a
magnos plus minus centum, quemadmodum Cassandra
occidit filios suos, et pueri mortui jacent sic ut vivere
putes. Habeo capides mille, quas reliquit patrono meo
Mummius, ubi Daedalus Niobam in equum Trojanum includit.
Nam Hermerotis pugnas et Petraitis in poculis habeo –
omnia ponderosa. Meum enim intellegere nulla pecunia
vendo."

51b

Collisa, dented
vasum aeneum, a bronze vase
martiolum (acc.), a little hammer
*sinus ūs m, a curve, fold, or
    hollow; the curved fold of the
    toga across the breast, which
    was used as a pocket; hence,
    pocket, breast, bosom, or lap
otio, nonchalantly

51c

solium (acc.) Jovis, the throne of
    Jupiter – i.e. the pinnacle of
    success.
Numquid alius, Does anyone else
    in the world . . . ?
condituram (acc.), process (for
    the making)
decollari, to be beheaded
pro luto, dirt-cheap – Trimalchio
    gives an economic reason. It
    is much more probable that the
    Emperor acted out of supersti-
tious fear of what seemed to
him a dangerous kind of
magical power.

52a

studiosus (nom.), an expert
scyphos (acc.), beakers
Cassandra – Trimalchio matches
    confusion in mythology with
    confusion in expression; he
    means silver beakers embossed
    with scenes showing how
    Medea . . .
capides (acc.), jugs
Daedalus, etc. – Niobe is con-
    fused with Pasiphaë, and the
    Trojan Horse with Daedalus'
    wooden cow!
includit, is shutting up
Hermeros, Petraites – Famous
    gladiators.
in poculis, (portrayed) on cups
ponderosa, heavy stuff
Meum intellegere, my knowledge
    (of silverware?)

Ceterum laudatus Trimalchio hilarius bibit, et jam   52b
ebrio proximus, "Nemo," inquit, "vestrum rogat
Fortunatam meam ut saltet? Credite mihi, cordacem
nemo melius ducit." Atque ipse, erectis super frontem
manibus, Syrum histrionem imitabatur, cantante tota
familia: "Madeia perimadeia!"

Et prodisset in medium, nisi Fortunata ad aurem ac-
cessisset; credo, dixerit non decere gravitatem ejus tam
humiles ineptias. Nihil autem tam inaequale erat; nam
modo Fortunatam verebatur, modo ad naturam suam
revertebatur.

Petauristarii autem tandem venerunt. Baro insulsissi-   53
mus cum scalis constitit, puerumque jussit per gradus et
in summa parte odaria saltare, circulos deinde ardentes
transilire et dentibus amphoram sustinere.

Mirabatur haec solus Trimalchio dicebatque ingratum
artificium esse, ceterum duo esse in rebus humanis quae
libentissime spectaret, petauristarios et cornicines;
reliqua acroamata tricas meras esse.

Dum haec dicit, puer petauristarius delapsus, in   54a
bracchium Trimalchionis cecidit. Conclamavit familia,

---

*hilarē (cp. *hilaritās), gayly,
   merrily
bibit, drank
*ēbrius a um, drunk, drunken
salto are, dance
cordacem ducit, does a strip
   tease
Syrum histrionem, Syrus the actor
*imitor ārī ātus sum, imitate
Madeia perimadeia, Yo ho ho and
   a big bravo! – Scholars do not
   know what *madeia perimadeia*
   means. Probably Trimalchio
   neither knew nor cared.
non decere . . . ineptias, that
   such low-brow nonsense was
   beneath his dignity
inaequale, erratic (as Trimalchio)

Petauristarius ī m, acrobat
Baro . . . scalis, a brainless big
   husky with a ladder
gradus (acc.), rungs
odaria saltare, to do a song-and-
   dance routine
circulos transilire, to jump
   through hoops
*ārdeō ēre ārsī ārsūrus, burn
cornicines (acc.), trumpeters
acroamata (acc.), amusements
tricas meras (acc.), silly
   nonsense

delapsus, slipped (and)
bracchium ī n, arm

nec minus convivae, non propter hominem tam putidum,
cujus et cervices fractas libenter vidissent, sed propter
malum exitum cenae, ne necesse haberent alienum mortuum
plorare. Ipse Trimalchio cum graviter ingemuisset
superque bracchium tamquam laesum incubuisset, concurrere
medici, et inter primos Fortunata, crinibus passis,
miseramque se atque infelicem proclamavit.

Nam puer quidem, qui ceciderat, circumibat jam   54b
dudum pedes nostros et missionem rogabat. Pessime
mihi erat ne his precibus per ridiculum aliquid catastrophae quaereretur. Adhuc enim memineram coci illius
qui oblitus fuerat porcum exinterare. Itaque totum cir-
cumspicere triclinium coepi, ne per parietem automatum
aliquod exiret, utique postquam servus verberari coepit,
qui bracchium domini alba potius quam conchyliata
involverat lana. Nec longe aberravit suspicio mea; in
vicem enim poenae venit decretum Trimalchionis, quo
puerum jussit liberum esse, ne quis posset dicere
tantum virum esse a servo vulneratum.

Comprobamus nos factum, et quam in praecipiti res   55
humanae essent, vario sermone loquimur. "Ita,"

---

putidus a um, putrid, nasty
ingemuisset, had groaned
laesum, injured
*incumbō ere cubuī cubitus, lean
  (Cp. *discumbō)
crinibus passis, her hair flying
  loose
*īnfēlīx īcis, unfortunate

54b

*jam dudum, long before this —
  With this expression the imperfect has the meaning of the
  pluperfect.
missionem (acc.), a reprieve
pessime mihi erat, I was on pins
  and needles
per ridiculum, in a comic vein
aliquid catastrophae, some

theatrical stunt
exinterare, to dress
per parietem, through the wall
automatum (nom.), surprise
verberari, to be beaten
potius, rather
conchyliata (abl.), purple
*aberrō āre āvī (ab + *errō),
  wander off, go astray, get out
  of place
in vicem, instead
decretum (nom.), decree

55

in praecipiti, on a brink — i.e.
  apt to fall. *Praecipiti* and
  casum (below) apply both
  literally and figuratively.

77

inquit Trimalchio, "non oportet hunc casum sine inscriptione transire," statimque codicillos poposcit et non diu cogitatione distorta, haec recitavit:

"Quód non éxpectés, ex tránsversó fit ubíque,
nóstra et súpra nós Fortúna negótia cúrat.
Quáre dá nobís vína Falérna, puér."

Ab hoc epigrammate coepit poetarum esse mentio, diuque summa carminis penes Mopsum Thracem memorata est.

"Quod autem," inquit Trimalchio, "putamus secundum 56a litteras difficillimum esse artificium? Ego puto medicum et nummularium: medicus, qui scit quid homunciones intra corpora sua habeant et quando febris veniat, etiam si illos odi pessime, quod mihi jubent saepe anatinam parari; nummularius, qui per argentum aes videt.

"Nam mutae bestiae laboriosissimae sunt boves et 56b oves: boves quorum beneficio panem manducamus; oves quod lana illae nos gloriosos faciunt. Et facinus indignum, aliquis ovillam est et tunicam habet! Apes enim ego divinas bestias puto; quae mel vomunt, etiam si

---

inscriptione (abl.), epigram
codicillos (acc. pl.), a writing-
  tablet
cogitatione distorta, racking his
  brains — Literally? English
  cognates?
ex transverso, unexpectedly
ubique, everywhere
nostra — Goes with *negotia*.
Falerna, Falernian — The very
  best wine.
summa . . . memorata est, pre-
  ëminence in poetry was ac-
  corded Mopsus, the Thracian —
  Mopsus was probably a gladiator who made a hobby of
  poetry!

56a

*secundum (+ acc.), next to,
  beside

nummularius ī m, banker
homunciones (nom.), folks
quando, when
febris (nom.), fever
odi, I hate
anatinam (acc.), duck
aes (acc.), copper — Used in
  counterfeit coins.

56b

*bōs bovis m or f, ox, bull, cow
oves, sheep
manducamus, we munch, eat —
  Oxen were used for ploughing
  and for threshing grain.
facinus, crime — Acc. of exclama-
  tion.
ovillam ēst, eats mutton
Apes (acc.), bees
quae mel vomunt, they spew
  honey

dicuntur illud a Jove afferre. Ideo autem pungunt,
quia ubicumque dulce est, ibi et acidum invenies."

pungunt, they sting ubicumque, wherever dulce, acidum, something sweet (honey), something bitter	(sting) — Trimalchio proves himself as good a philosopher as a poet.

Written Exercise 50-56

1 (After they had) merrily given applause, they all shouted, "Good
luck to you!"
2 A silver crown had been given to the cook because of course the
guests, who were all drunk, thought that he was a good cook.
3 They say that the man took ten gold denarii out of his pocket.
4 To the boy I shall say, "Imitate your father."
5 To the girls I shall say, "Imitate your mother."
6 Do you not know that your house is burning?
7 Don't lean over the couch!
8 Long before this the boy had been begging (imperfect) not to be
sent home.
9 I believe that the white cow has wandered off out of the field into
the wood.
10 Beside the road many soldiers lay dead.
11 He will ask why the cook has poured out this wine.
12 If I were so unfortunate, I would not want *(nōlō)* to live.

Jam etiam philosophos de negotio dejiciebat.   57a

Ceterum Ascyltos, intemperantis licentiae, cum omnia,
sublatis manibus, eluderet et usque ad lacrimas rideret,
unus ex collibertis Trimalchionis excanduit, is ipse qui
supra me discumbebat, et "Quid rides," inquit, "berbex?
An tibi non placent lautitiae domini mei? Tu enim beatior
es et convivare melius soles. Ego si secundum illum

57a
 	
Ascyltos (nom.) — See page 37.
intemperantis licentiae, (a man)
  of uninhibited impulsiveness —
  Literally?
eluderet, was making fun of
lacrimas (acc.), tears
excanduit, flared up
berbex, you zilly ass — *Berbex,*
	mispronunciation of *vervex,*
	  wether.
	beatior, wealthier
	convivare, to socialize — Bad
	  English, bad Latin; *convivare*
	  should be deponent.
	illum — Refers to Ascyltos and is
	  addressed to the other guests.
	  Be prepared for similar shifts
	  below.

discumberem, jam illi balatum cluxissem. Bellum
pomum, qui rideatur alios!

"Quid habet quod rideat? Eques Romanus es! Et ego   57b
regis filius. 'Quare ergo servus factus es?' Quia ipse
me dedi in servitutem et malui civis Romanus esse quam
tributarius. Et nunc spero me sic vivere ut nemini jocus
sim. Homo inter homines sum. Capite aperto ambulo.
Assem nemini debeo. Constitutum habui numquam. Nemo
mihi in foro dixit, 'Redde quod debes'. Glebulas emi.
Lamellulas paravi. Viginti ventres pasco et canem.
Contubernalem meam redemi, ne quis in sinu illius manus
tergeret. Mille denarios pro capite solvi. Sevir gratis
factus sum. Spero sic moriar ut mortuus non erubescam.

"Tu autem tam laboriosus es ut post te non respicias?   57c

---

balatum cluxissem, I would have
  throttled his braying — Lit.
  bleating.
Bellum pomum, (He thinks himself) some punkins! — Lit. a
  pretty fruit.
rideatur — What mistake in Latin
  is this?

57b

eques Romanus, a Roman knight
  — Ascyltos wears a gold ring,
  a privilege of the knights, indicative of their high social
  status. The speaker assumes
  that Ascyltos' ring is phony.
tributarius, a (royal) tax-payer —
  Rome sometimes allowed petty
  kings to reign, subject to her
  and paying taxes. Here however the speaker is merely
  matching pretense with
  pretense.
jocus ī m, a joke
Constitutum (diem), a summons —
  Lit. a day fixed (for appearance in court).

Glebulas (acc.), a bit of land
Lamellulas (acc.), a bit of ready
  cash
ventres (acc.), bellies
pasco, I feed
contubernalis is m or f, his
  woman, her man — Used of
  slaves as sex partners, originally of soldiers as tent-
  mates.
pro capite = pro libertate mea —
  He brought himself free.
Sevir, a priest of the Emperor
  cult
gratis, without paying (the usual
  fees)
erubescam, I shall blush

57c

respicias — Reference to a fable:
  everyone carries his faults in
  a bag *behind* him so that each
  sees another's faults but not
  his own.

In alio peduclum vides; in te ricinum non vides. Tibi
soli ridiclei videmur. Ecce magister tuus, homo major
natus; placemus illi. Tu lacticulosus, nec mu nec ma
argutas, vasus fictilis, immo lorus in aqua, lentior, non
melior. Tu beatior es? Bis prande, bis cena! Ego fidem
meam malo quam thesauros. Ad summam, quisquam me
bis poposcit? Annis quadraginta servus fui; nemo tamen
sciit utrum servus essem an liber.

"Et puer capillatus in hanc coloniam veni. Adhuc   57d
basilica non erat facta. Dedi tamen operam ut domino
satis facerem, homini maijesto et dignitosso, cujus
pluris erat unguis quam tu totus es. Et habebam in domo
qui mihi pedem opponerent hac illac. Tamen − genio
illius gratias − enatavi. Haec sunt vera athla; nam
liberum nasci tam facile est quam 'Accede istoc.' Quid
nunc stupes tamquam hircus in ervilia?"

Post hoc dictum Giton, qui ad pedes nostros stabat,   58a
risum jam diu compressum etiam indecenter effudit. Quod

Peduclum (acc.), a louse

ricinum (acc.), a tick − A parasite of sheep, etc.

ridiclei, ridiclous − Petronius
  makes the speaker ridiculous
  by the very way he pronounces
  the word.

magister, teacher − i.e. Agamemnon.

major natus, older than you − But
  the speaker says *natus* for
  natu, another "ridiclous"
  error. Cp. 47c.

Tu lacticulosus . . . melior,
  You're just an itsy-bitsy baby
  boy, can't say boo to a goose,
  weak as a clay pot − I mean
  flabby as leather in water −
  not a bit better.

beatior, wealthier

prande (imperative), take
  breakfast

thesauros (acc. pl.), a mint of
  money

57d

basilica (nom.), the town hall

maijesto et dignitosso (dat.),
  honorious and respectified −
  Vulgar word formations.
  English cognates?

unguis (nom.), finger nail

qui mihi . . . illac, (rivals) who
  tried to trip me up here and
  there − Literally?

enatavi, I swam to land − i.e.
  gained favor.

athla (neut.), struggles

accede istoc, (saying) 'Come
  here'

Quid . . . ervilia, Why are you
  staring at me now, like a goat
  in a bean patch?

58a

pedes − Giton, in the rôle of
  their personal slave, stood at

cum animadvertisset adversarius Ascylti, flexit convicium
in puerum et "Tu autem," inquit, "etiam tu rides, caepa
cirrata? Io Saturnalia! Rogo, mensis December est?
Nescit quid faciat. Plane qualis est dominus, talis et
servus.

"Vix me teneo, nec sum natura caldicerebrius, sed   58b
cum coepi, matrem meam dupundii non facio. Recte,
videbo te in publicum, mus, immo terrae tuber. Nec
sursum nec deorsum non cresco, nisi dominum tuum in
rutae folium non conjeci. Nec tibi parsero, licet mehercules
Jovem Olympium clames.

"Non didici geometrias, critica, et alogias nenias,   58c
sed lapidarias litteras scio, partes centum dico. Eamus
in forum et pecunias mutuemur. Jam scies hoc ferrum
fidem habere. Vah, bella res est volpis uda. Ita lucrum

---

the point where Encolpius'
and Ascyltos' feet protruded
over the back edge of the
couch.
flexit convicium, he turned his
  abuse
caepa cirrata, you curly-headed
  little stinker — Lit. curly
  onion.
Io Saturnalia, Hurrah for the
  Feast of Saturn! — A December
  festival, during which there
  was much festive nonsense
  and slaves were allowed to be
  saucy.
qualis — talis et, as — so also

58b

caldicerebrius (nom.), hot-headed
dupundii non facio, I don't care
  two cents for — Lit. I don't regard her as worth two cents
  (gen.).
Recte, O.K.! — Said with a
  threatening sneer.
terrae tuber, toadstool
sursum — deorsum, up — down
in rutae folium, give a big dose

of saltpeter — Lit. into a leaf
of rue, which was supposed to
inhibit sexual vigor. (Cp.
Waters on 37, 19.)
parsero, I shall have mercy
licet, even if

58c

critica . . . nenias, criticism and
  such senseless twaddle
lapidarias, capital — Capitals
  were used for inscriptions, fine
  books, etc.
partes centum, table of percen-
  tages (interest rates)
mutuemur, let's try to borrow
ferrum — The speaker displays
  his iron ring. Unlike Ascyltos,
  he cannot wear a gold ring as
  a badge of status, but "a
  man's a man for a' that."
Vah, Aha! — Giton's eyes have
  betrayed his discomfiture.
volpis uda (nom.), a wet fox
lucrum (acc.), profit — In this
  sentence the speaker gets all
  tangled up. See if you can un-
  scramble his thought, by making

faciam et ita bene moriar ut populus per exitum meum
juret, nisi te ubique, toga perversa, fuero persecutus.
Bella res et iste qui te haec docet, mufrius, non
magister . . ."

Coeperat Ascyltos respondere, sed Trimalchio delec-   59a
tatus colliberti eloquentia, "Agite," inquit, "scordalias
de medio! Suaviter sit potius, et tu, Hermeros, parce
adulescentulo. Sanguen illi fervet. Tu melior esto.
Semper in hac re qui vincitur vincit. Et tu cum esses
capo, coco coco, aeque cor non habebas. Simus ergo,
quod melius est, a primitiis hilares, et Homeristas
spectemus."

Intravit factio statim hastisque scuta concrepuit. Ipse
Trimalchio in pulvino consedit, et cum Homeristae
Graecis versibus colloquerentur, ut insolenter solent, ille
canora voce Latine legebat librium.

Mox silentio facto, "Scitis," inquit, "quam fabulam   59b
agant? Diomedes et Ganymedes duo fratres fuerunt.

---

a strictly literal translation;
it can scarcely be sillier than
the original.
ubique, everywhere
toga perversa, with your toga
  upside down (?) — Scholars
  don't even agree whose toga is
  meant.
mufrius, non magister, a tinker,
  not a teacher

59a

scordalias, squabbling
potius, rather, instead
Hermeros — The guest who has
  just finished speaking.
Sanguen . . . fervet, His blood
  boils — i.e. He is hot-blooded.
capo, coco coco, a cocky young
  cock-a-doodle-doo
cor (acc.), good sense — Lit.
  heart.
a primitiis, all over again

*hilaris e, gay, merry (cp.
  *hilaritās)
Homeristas (acc.), Homeric
  actors
factio (nom.), the troupe (of
  actors)
concrepuit, banged
in pulvino consedit, sat up on a
  cushion
ut . . . solent, as their unusual
  custom usually is — Literally?
canorus a um, sing-song
Latine, in Latin — Trimalchio
  follows the story with a
  translation.

59b

Diomedes — For this passage
  you need your dictionary of
  mythology. Try to make better
  use of it than Trimalchio did
  of his.

Horum soror erat Helena. Agamemnon illam rapuit et
Dianae cervam subjecit. Ita nunc Homeros dicit
quemadmodum inter se pugnent Trojani et Parentini.
Vicit scilicet et Iphigeniam, filiam suam, Achilli dedit
uxorem. Ob eam rem Ajax insanit et statim argumentum
explicabit.''

Haec ut dixit Trimalchio, clamorem Homeristae sus-   59c
tulerunt, interque familiam discurrentem vitulus in
lance ducenaria elixus allatus est, et quidem galeatus.
Secutus est Ajax, strictoque gladio, tamquam insaniret,
concidit, ac modo versa modo supina gesticulatus, gladio
frusta collegit mirantibusque convivis divisit.

Nec diu mirari licuit tam elegantes strophas. Nam   60a
repente lacunaria sonare coeperunt totumque triclinium
intremuit. Conterritus ego exsurrexi et timui ne per
tectum petauristarius aliquis descenderet. Nec minus
reliqui convivae mirantes sustulerunt vultus, expectantes
quid novi de caelo nuntiaretur. Ecce autem diductis
lacunaribus, subito circulus ingens demittitur, cujus per

Dianae . . . subjecit, he put a
deer under Diana — Literal
translation is preferable because it best represents the
idea the words must have suggested to the guests. Scholarly attempts to make more
"sense" here are beside the
point.
Homeros — Greek nominative
Parentini — You don't know what
people Trimalchio means, but
don't worry — no one else does.
insanire, to go, or be, crazy —
Homer does not tell the story,
but Ajax did go crazy, and
mistaking some sheep for
enemies, he put them to the
sword.
argumentum explicabit, will give
us the finale of the play
vitulus . . . elixus, a boiled calf
on a two hundred pound platter
galeatus, with a helmet on its
head — To make sure that

"Ajax" will mistake it for an
enemy warrior!
concidit, he slashed away (at the
calf)
versa (manu), with hand turned
down — i.e. with the edge of
the blade.
supina (manu), with hand turned
up — i.e. with the *back* of the
blade, which would not cut a
thing! This *proves* that he is
crazy.
frusta (acc.), slices

60a

strophas (acc.), tricks
lacunar aris n, ceiling panel
*sonō āre uī itus, make a sound
or a noise (Cp. *sonus)
intremuit, shook
*exsurgō ere surrēxī (ex + *surgō),
rise up, get up (from table)
petauristarius (nom.), acrobat
circulus (nom.), a hoop

totum orbem coronae aureae cum alabastris unguenti
pendebant. Haec apophoreta jubemur sumere.
Jam in mensa repositorium cum placentis aliquot erat   60b
positum. Quod medium Priapus a pistore factus tenebat,
gremioque satis amplo omnis generis poma sustinebat
more vulgato. Avidius ad pompam manus extendimus, et
repente nova ludorum missio hilaritatem hic refecit.
Omnes enim placentae omniaque poma, etiam minima
vexatione contacta, coeperunt effundere crocum, et
usque ad os molestus umor accidere.

Rati ergo sacrum esse ferculum tam religioso apparatu   60c
perfusum, consurreximus altius et, "Augusto, patri patriae,
feliciter," diximus. Quibusdam tamen etiam post hanc
venerationem poma rapientibus, nos ipsi mappas im-
plevimus, ego praecipue, qui nullo satis amplo munere
putabam me onerare Gitonis sinum.

---

orbem (acc.), circumference
alabastris (abl.), alabaster
  bottles
apophoreta (neut.), as dinner
  gifts – It was customary to
  give presents to dinner guests.

60b

placenta ae f, cooky
Priapus . . . factus, a Priapus
  made by the baker – A pastry
  figure of the phallic god of
  fruitfulness.
gremio (abl.), lap – A euphemism,
  even more so in English because Priapus is *not* sitting
  down.
pomum ī n, fruit
vulgato (abl.), usual – See
  Priapus in the Encyclopaedia
  Britannica.
pompam (acc.), his magnificent
  display
ludorum missio (nom.), round of
  sport

vexatione (abl.), pressure
crocum (acc.), (a vapor of)
  saffron – Saffron was used for
  food seasoning, perfumery,
  hair tonic, medicine, and in
  religious rituals.
umor (nom.), vapor
accidere, reached – Historical
  infinitive.

60c

*reor rērī ratus sum, think,
  suppose
consurreximus altius, we rose
  from the table and stood up
  straight
Augusto (dat.), the Emperor – It
  was a religious custom at ban-
  quets to bless the *genius* of
  the Emperor.
venerationem (acc.), solemnity
mappas (acc.), napkins – Guests
  took dinner gifts *(apophoreta)*
  home, wrapped in their napkins.

Inter haec Trimalchio ad Nicerotem respexit et, 61a
"Solebas," inquit, "suavius esse in convictu. Nescio
quid nunc taces. Oro te, sic felicem me videas, narra
illud quod tibi usu venit." Niceros delectatus affabilitate
amici, "Omne me," inquit, "lucrum transeat, nisi jam
dudum gaudimonio dissilio, quod te talem video. Itaque
hilaria mera sint, etsi timeo istos scholasticos, ne me
rideant. Narrabo tamen. Quid enim mihi aufert qui ridet?
Satius est rideri quam derideri."

Haec ubi dicta dedit, talem fabulam exorsus est: 61b
"Cum adhuc servus essem, habitabamus in Vico Angusto.
Nunc Gavillae domus est. Ibi, quomodo dei volunt, amare
coepi uxorem Terentii coponis. Noveratis Melissam
Tarentinam, pulcherrimum bacciballum. Sed ego non
mehercules corporaliter illam aut propter res venerias
curavi, sed magis quod benemoria fuit. Si quid ab illa
petivi, numquam mihi negatum. Fecit assem, semissem

61a

in convictu, at a party
sic . . . videas, as proof that you
  like to see me happy — There
  is just the slightest hint that
  Niceros' silence is due to envy.
*fēlīx īcis, fortunate, happy,
  prosperous (Cp. *fēlīciter,
  *īnfēlīx)
usu venit, actually occurred —
  i.e. that true story of yours.
lucrum i n, profit, wealth
gaudimonio dissilio, I've been
  a-bustin' with happiness
talem, in such fine fettle
merus a um, undiluted, pure
scholasticos (acc.), educated
  fellows — Agamemnon et al.
Satius . . . derideri, It's more fun
  to get someone to laugh at you
  than to let someone get the
  laugh on you.

61b

talem, the following
exorsus est, he began — In this
  sentence epic diction is used
  with whimsical effect.
in Vico Angusto, on Narrow
  Avenue
Gavillae — Dat. of possession
Terentii coponis, of Terentius,
  the innkeeper — Terentius is a
  slave who manages an inn for
  his master.
Melissam Tarentinam (acc.),
  Melissa (Honeybee) of
  Tarentum
bacciballum (acc.), little roly-
  poly
res venerias (acc.), sexual
  attraction
benemoria (fem. nom.), a good
  sport
semissem, half an as, a half-
  penny

habui. Quicquid habui, in illius sinum demandavi. Nec umquam fefellitus sum.

"Hujus contubernalis ad villam supremum diem obiit.   61c
Itaque per scutum per ocream egi aginavi quemadmodum
ad illam pervenirem. Scitis autem, in angustiis amici
apparent.

---

demandavi, I entrusted
fefellitus sum, I was cheated

61c

Hujus contubernalis — i.e.
Terentius. See on *contubernalis*, 57b.

supremum . . . obiit, he drew his
last breath, he passed away
per scutum . . . aginavi, I
schemed and dreamed by hook
or crook
in angustiis, in emergences

Written Exercise 57-61

As the starting point for each of the following, study the word
given in parentheses as used in the passage indicated.

1 (*hilarēs*, 59a) "So let's be merry! Let all the guests be merry!"
Thus we spoke (while) dining merrily, but there were several
guests who did not like our merriment.
2 (*sonāre*, 60a) Suddenly the table itself began to make a noise. I
did not know why it was making a noise, but I clearly heard the
noise.
3 (*exsurrēxī*, 60a) I (for my part) got up (from the table) in a panic.
I noticed that some other guests, (who were) also panic-stricken,
were getting up to see what was happening.
4 (*ratī*, *cōnsurrēximus altius*, 60c) So, thinking that this dish was
sacred to the gods, the women rose (from the table and stood up)
straight. I however do not think that the dish was sacred to the
gods. My father thinks so. What do you think?
5 (*fēlīcem*, 61a) I want to see you (singular) happy. May you not be
unhappy! Good luck to you all!

"Forte dominus Capuam exierat ad scruta scita ex-ₗ   62a
pedienda. Nactus ego occasionem, persuadeo hospitem

62a

Capuam (acc.) — A town in south-
west Italy

ad scruta . . . expedienda, to
pull some slick deal
hospitem (acc.), a guest — Normal
case usage?

nostrum ut mecum ad quintum miliarium veniat. Erat autem miles, fortis tamquam Orcus. Apoculamus nos circa gallicinia. Luna lucebat tamquam meridie.

"Venimus intra monumenta. Homo meus coepit ad   62b
stelas facere. Sedeo ego cantabundus et stelas numero. Deinde ut respexi ad comitem, ille exuit se, et omnia vestimenta secundum viam posuit. Mihi anima in naso esse. Stabam tamquam mortuus. At ille circumminxit vestimenta sua, et subito lupus factus est. Nolite me jocari putare. Ut mentiar, nullius patrimonium tanti facio. Sed quod coeperam dicere, postquam lupus factus est, ululare coepit et in silvas fugit.

"Ego primitus nesciebam ubi essem. Deinde accessi   62c
ut vestimenta ejus tollerem. Illa autem lapidea facta sunt. Qui mori timore nisi ego? Gladium tamen strinxi et in tota via umbras cecidi, donec ad villam amicae meae

---

miliarium (acc.), milestone
Apoculamus . . . gallicinia, We
  skedaddled out of the house
  about cockcrow — i.e. long
  before dawn.

62b

*monumentum ī n, monument,
  tomb — Highways were lined
  with tombs just beyond city
  limits.
ad stelas facere, to have a do by
  some gravestones — To use
  the cemetery as a rest room.
*sedeō ēre sēdī sessus, sit, sit
  down
cantabundus (nom.), humming the
  time away
exuit, undressed
Mihi . . . esse, I practically
  stopped breathing — *Anima
  ae f, the power to breathe.
  With his last breath, through
  mouth or nose, a man's *anima*,
  "soul," departs and he dies.

Lit. Niceros says: My breath
  was *(esse*, historical infinitive)
  in my nose, i.e. on the point of
  departure. Cp. on *Chrysanthus*,
  42a.
circumminxit, made a ring of
  urine around — Such a "magic
  circle" was supposed to pre-
  vent theft.
lupus (predic. nom.), a wolf
jocor ārī, joke
*mentior īrī mentītus sum, lie,
  tell a lie
facio — See on *pili*, 44e, and
  dupundii, 58b.
ululare, to howl

62c

lapideus a um, stone — He could
  not budge them. The magic
  circle was effective!
Qui mori = Quis umquam mortuus
  est?
umbras (acc. pl.), every shadow
donec, until

pervenirem. Ut larva intravi. Paene animam ebullivi.
Sudor mihi per bifurcum volabat. Oculi mortui. Vix
umquam refectus sum.

"Melissa mea mirari coepit quod tam sero ambularem,   62d
et 'Si ante,' inquit, 'venisses, saltem nobis adjuvisses.
Lupus enim villam intravit et omnia pecora perculit; tamquam lanius sanguinem illis misit. Nec tamen derisit,
etiam si fugit. Servus enim noster lancea collum ejus
trajecit.'

"Haec ut audivi, operire oculos amplius non potui,   62e
sed clara luce Gai nostri domum fugi tamquam copo compilatus, et postquam veni in illum locum in quo lapidea
vestimenta erant facta, nihil inveni nisi sanguinem. Ut
vero domum veni, jacebat miles meus in lecto tamquam
bovis, et collum ejus medicus curabat. Intellexi illum
versipellem esse. Nec postea cum illo panem gustare
potui, non si me occidisses. Viderint alii quid de hoc
exopinissent; ego si mentior, genios vestros iratos habeam."

Attonitis admiratione universis, "Si qua fides est,"   63a
inquit Trimalchio, "ut mihi pili inhorruerunt, quia scio

Ut larva, like a ghost
ebullivi — See on *Mihi . . . esse,*
  62b.
Sudor . . . volabat, The sweat
  was streaming (Literally?)
  down my crotch

62d

sero, late (at night)
saltem, at least
Lupus (nom.), a wolf
perculit, worried
lanius (nom.), a butcher
sanguis inis m, blood
misit, he let, he shed
lancea, with a spear

62e

operire, to close — Niceros was

too upset to sleep.
Gai = domini — See on *Fortunata,*
  37a.
copo compilatus, a huckster who's
  been swindled (and is running
  after the swindler)
*lectus ī m, bed, couch
versipellem, a werewolf — Predi-
  cate acc.
Viderint . . . exopinissent, Other
  people may think what they
  like about this
*īrāscor ī īrātus sum (+ dat.), be
  angry

63a

Attonitus a um, astounded
Si qua . . . inhorruerunt, By all
  that's holy, my hair stood on
  end

Niceronem nihil nugarum narrare. Immo certus est et
minime linguosus. Nam et ipse vobis rem horribilem
narrabo.

"Cum adhuc capillatus essem, Gai nostri delicatus   63b
mortuus est, mehercules margaritum, zacritus et omnium
numerum. Cum ergo illum mater misella ploraret et nos
tum plures in tristimonio essemus, subito strigae stridere
coeperunt. Putares canem leporem persequi.

"Habebamus tunc hominem Cappadocem, longum,   63c
valde audaculum, et qui valebat. Poterat bovem iratum
tollere. Hic audacter stricto gladio, extra januam
procucurrit, involuta sinistra manu curiose, et mulierem
tamquam hoc loco — salvum sit quod tango — mediam
trajecit. Audimus gemitum, et — plane non mentiar —
ipsas non vidimus.

"Baro autem noster cum intrasset se projecit in lec-   63d
tum, et corpus totum lividum habebat quasi flagellis

---

nugae ārum f, nonsense
linguosus (nom.), a bluffer, liar
— Literally?

63b

delicatus (nom.), favorite (slave
 boy)
margaritum . . . numerum, a perfect jewel, 'e was, one in a
 million, perfection personified
*misellus a um, poor little, poor
 old — Diminutive of *miser.*
plures, quite a number of us — Cp.
 fortior, quite or rather brave
in tristimonio, sharing her sorrow
strigae (nom.), witches
stridere, to screech
leporem (acc.), a hare

63c

Cappadocem — Cappadocian
 slaves were known for their
 strength.
curiose, carefully
*salvus a um, safe, unharmed,
 alive — Trimalchio presses his
 finger into his stomach to show
 the way the sword entered the
 witch's body *(mulierem),* but
 immediately deprecates the act
 because he might suffer sim-
 ilar harm through magical
 identification with her.
gemitum, a groan

63d

Baro (nom.), brawny athlete —
 i.e. the Cappadocian.
quasi, as if
flagellis, with lashes

caesus, quia scilicet illum tetigerat mala manus. Nos clusa janua redimus iterum ad officium, sed dum mater amplexaret corpus filii sui, tangit et videt manuciolum de stramentis factum. Non cor habebat, non intestina, non quicquam. Scilicet jam puerum strigae abstulerant et supposuerant stramenticium vavatonem.

"Rogo vos, oportet credatis: sunt mulieres plussciae,   63e sunt nocturnae, et quod sursum est deorsum faciunt. Ceterum baro ille longus post hoc factum numquam coloris sui fuit. Immo post paucos dies phreneticus periit."

---

mala (nom.), evil — i.e. the witch's.
clusa (abl.), shut, locked
iterum, again
amplexaret, went to put her arms around
manuciolum . . . factum, a dummy made of straw
cor (acc.), heart
strigae (nom.) the witches
stramenticium vavatonem (acc.), a straw puppet

63e

plussciae, that know too much, uncanny
nocturnae, those that prowl around at night
sursum — deorsum, up — down — They get everything topsy-turvy. In this passage Trimalchio does not distinguish *mulieres* from *strigae;* he slyly blends cynicism with his superstition.
phreneticus, in a fit of delirium

Written Exercise 62, 63

As the starting point for each of the following, study the word given in parentheses as used in the passage indicated.

1 *(monumenta,* 62b) He said that he had seen many tombs beside that road. Did you not see them?

2 *(sedeō,* 62b) A man asked me why I was sitting looking at the tombs. I replied that my family did not possess a tomb.

3 *(anima in nāsō,* 62b) The man said that his *anima* was in his nose because he was so frightened that he thought he was going to die. But neither *anima* nor *genius* can be translated into our language.

4 *(mentiar,* 62b) You cannot persuade me to (tell a) lie. Do not suppose that I have lied. I cannot lie because of course I am a friend of Trimalchio's.

5 *(lectō,* 62e) The soldier was lying in his bed, and he was unwilling to get up. When I asked him why he was lying in bed, he replied that he thought that it was a good (thing) to lie in bed.

6 (īrātōs, 62e) If I (am telling a) lie, may I have all the gods angry
(with me)! Do not be angry with your father. (Although he was)
angry, he denied that he was angry.

7 (misella, 63b) Have you not learned both misellus and miser?
You don't suppose that these two words are the same, (do you)?

8 (salvum, 63c) May our friends be unharmed! May they reach Rome
unharmed!

Miramur nos et pariter credimus, osculatique mensam   64a
rogamus nocturnas ut suis se teneant, dum redimus a
cena.

Et sane jam lucernae mihi plures videbantur ardere totumque triclinium esse mutatum, cum Trimalchio ad
delicias suas respexit, quem Croesum appellabat. Puer
autem lippus, sordissimis dentibus, catellam nigram atque
indecenter pinguem prasina involvebat fascia, panemque
semissem ponebat super torum atque nausea recusantem
saginabat. Quo admonitus officii Trimalchio Scylacem
jussit adduci, "praesidium domus familiaeque."

Nec mora, ingentis formae adductus est canis catena   64b
vinctus, admonitusque ostiarii calce ut cubaret, ante
mensam se posuit. Tum Trimalchio, jactans panem,
"Nemo," inquit, "in domo mea me plus amat." Indig-
natus puer, quod Scylacem tam effuse laudaret, catellam
in terram deposuit, hortatusque est ut ad rixam properaret.

64a

pariter, in like manner — Ironical,
  because both wonder and belief
  may, or may not, be sincere.
*ōsculor ārī ātus sum, kiss — To
  kiss the table is to "touch
  wood."
suis (dat.), to their own affairs —
  i.e. to mind their own business.
*lucerna ae f, lamp
delicias (acc.), pet slave boy —
  Cp. 28a.
lippus (nom.), blear-eyed
catella ae f, puppy
pinguem, fat — With catellam.
prasina fascia, with a green
  ribbon

panem semissem (acc.), half a
  loaf of bread — The pup had
  already eaten the other half.
saginabat, was trying to stuff —
  i.e. to force the pup to eat
  more.
Scylax acis, Tiny — Trimalchio's
  dog.

64b

catena vinctus, on a leash
ostiarii . . . cubaret, upon being
  kicked by the butler as a sign
  to lie down
jactans, tossing (him)
ad rixam, to (start) a fight

Scylax, canino scilicet usus ingenio, taeterrimo la- 64c
tratu triclinium implevit, Margaritamque Croesi paene
laceravit. Nec intra rixam tumultus constitit, sed candelabrum etiam super mensam eversum, et vasa omnia cry-
stallina comminuit et oleo ferventi aliquot convivas
sparsit.

Trimalchio, ne videretur jactura motus, basiavit pu- 64d
erum, ac jussit super dorsum ascendere suum. Non
moratus ille usus est equo, manuque plena scapulas ejus
subinde verberavit, interque risum proclamavit, "Bucca,
Bucca, quot sunt hic?"

Inter haec triclinii valvas lictor percussit, amictus- 65a
que veste alba, cum ingenti frequentia comissator intravit.
Ego majestate conterritus praetorem putabam venisse.
Itaque temptavi assurgere et nudos pedes in terram deferre.

64c

ingenio (abl.), nature
taeterrimo latratu, with the most
  abominable barking
Margaritam, Pearl — Name of the
  puppy.
intra rixam, with (Lit. within the
  limits of) a mere dog fight
candelabrum (nom.), a lamp
  stand
et . . . comminuit, both smashed
  all the crystal ware to
  pieces . . .
oleo ferventi, with hot oil

64d

jactura, by the loss (of the
  crystal)
*bāsiō āre āvī ātus, kiss
dorsum ī n, back
scapulas (acc.), shoulders
verberavit, he smacked
Bucca . . . hic — "In
  Cambridgeshire this game is
  still played. The rider holds
up his hand and says 'Buck,
buck, how many fingers do I
hold up?' The other has to act
as horse till he guesses cor-
rectly. (The guessing part
was called *micare digitis*:
44b)." — Sedgwick, *ad loc.*,
1925.

65a

valvas (acc.), door
lictor (nom.), lictor — An official
  bodyguard.
amictus (nom.), clothed
frequentia (abl.), throng of
  people
comissator (nom.), a late guest —
  More accurately, one who
  makes the rounds of drinking
  parties, a "playboy"; originally applied to riotous worship-
  ers in processions honoring the
  god of wine.
majestate, by his official status
praetorem (acc.), the governor
*assurgō ere surrēxī surrēctus
  (ad + *surgō), rise up, get up
  (from table)

Risit hanc trepidationem Agamemnon et, "Contine te,"
inquit, "homo stultissime. Habinnas sevir est, idemque
lapidarius, qui videtur monumenta optime facere."

Recreatus hoc sermone reposui cubitum, Habinnamque   65b
intrantem cum admiratione ingenti spectabam. Ille autem
jam ebrius uxoris suae umeris imposuerat manus, onera-
tusque aliquot coronis, et unguento per frontem in oculos
fluente, praetorio loco se posuit, continuoque vinum poposcit. Delectatus hac Trimalchio hilaritate, et ipse
capaciorem poposcit scyphum, quaesivitque quomodo
acceptus esset.

"Omnia," inquit Habinnas, "habuimus praeter te.   65c
Oculi enim mei hic erant. Et mehercules bene fuit.
Scissa lautum novemdiale servo suo misello faciebat,
quem mortuum manu miserat. Suaviter fuit, etiam si
coacti sumus dimidias potiones super ossucula ejus   (66)
effundere.

---

stultus a um, stupid
Habinnas . . . est, It is Habinnas, a priest of the Emperor
  cult — This priesthood was a
  relatively unimportant public
  office granted to freedmen,
  which gave them the right to
  have lictors. Habinnas in-
  sists on having his even at
  parties.
lapidarius (nom.), a stonecutter

65b

cubitum, elbow — See on *cubitum*,
  27b.
umerus ī m, shoulder
praetorio loco, in the place of
  honor (at table)
capaciorem scyphum (acc.), a
  bigger wine cup
acceptus esset, he had been
  treated — At the party from

which he has just come. Cp.
accepisset, 42c.

65c

hīc, here (with you) — A little
  folksy flattery.
Scissa (fem.) — A friend of
  Habinnas.
novemdiale (neut. acc.), funeral
  feast — Which ended *nine days*
  of mourning.
manu — See on *manu misit*, 42c.
  Ironical to free a slave when
  he dies! It was customary for
  a master to free slaves by will,
  upon his *own* death.
dimidius a um, half
ossucula (acc.), li'l ole bones —
  A diminutive *(ossiculum* from
  os, ossis, bone) slurred in
  pronunciation. Pouring wine
  over the dead is mentioned
  also in 77c.

"Sed narra mihi, Gai, rogo, Fortunata quare non 67a
discumbit?"

"Quomodo nosti," inquit, "illam," Trimalchio,
"nisi argentum composuerit, nisi reliquias pueris
diviserit, aquam in os suum non conjiciet."
"Atqui," respondit Habinnas, "nisi illa discumbit,
ego me apoculo." Et coeperat surgere, nisi signo dato,
Fortunata quater amplius a tota familia esset vocata.
Venit ergo, galbino succincta cingillo, ita ut infra cera-
sina appareret tunica et periscelides tortae phaecasiaeque
inauratae. Tunc sudario manus tergens, quod in collo
habebat, applicat se illi toro in quo Scintilla Habinnae
discumbebat uxor, osculataque plaudentem, "Est te,"
inquit, "videre?"

Eo deinde perventum est, ut Fortunata armillas suas 67b
crassissimis detraheret lacertis Scintillaeque miranti
ostenderet. Ultimo etiam periscelides resolvit et reticulum aureum, quem ex obrussa esse dicebat. Notavit haec
Trimalchio jussitque afferri omnia et, "Videtis," inquit,

67a

nosti, you know — shortened
  form of novisti
Atqui, but anyhow
ego me apoculo, I'll make myself
  scarce
nisi, (and would have done so)
  had not . . .
quater amplius, more than four
  times
galbino . . . cingillo, with her
  dress bloused up over a dainty
  yellow sash
infra, below it
cerasinus a um, cherry-red
periscelides tortae, spiral
  anklets
phaecasiae inauratae, gold
  trimmed white slippers
sudarium ī n, handkerchief
applicat, draped
Scintilla ae f, Sparkle

*plaudō ere sī sus, clap the
  hands, applaud
Est te videre, I've been just
  dying to see you, my dear — A
  conventional greeting: Is it
  (really possible) to get a look
  at you (after so long a time)?
  Context and tone of voice carry
  more of the meaning than the
  actual words.

67b

Eo . . . ut, Within minutes things
  had arrived at the point where
  . . . — Literally?
armilla ae f, bracelet
crassissimis lacertis (abl.), her
  very pudgy arms
reticulum ī n, hair net
ex obrussa, (made) of pure gold

"mulieris compedes. Sic nos barcalae despoliamur. Haec
armilla sex pondo et selibram debet habere. Et ipse nihilo minus habeo decem pondo armillam." Ultimo etiam,
ne mentiri videretur, stateram jussit afferri et circum-
latum approbari pondus.

Nec melior fuit Scintilla, quae de cervice sua cap-   67c
sellam detraxit aureolam, quam Felicionem appellabat.
Inde duo crotalia protulit, et Fortunatae in vicem con-
sideranda dedit et, "Domini," inquit, "mei beneficio nemo
habet meliora."

"Quid," inquit Habinnas, "excatarissasti me, ut tibi
emerem fabam vitream. Plane si filiam haberem, auriculas
illi praeciderem. Mulieres si non essent, omnia pro luto
haberemus."

Interim mulieres sauciae inter se riserunt ebriaeque   67d
junxerunt oscula, dum altera diligentiam matris familiae
jactat, altera delicias et indiligentiam viri. Dumque

---

compedes (acc.), shackles —
  Implying that women bind men
  down by requiring them to
  spend money on jewelry.
Sic . . . despoliamur, That's the
  way we stupid men get fleeced
sex . . . selibram, six and a half
  pounds (of gold) — A rather
  cumbersome bracelet even if
  the Roman pound was only
  7/10 of ours.
pondo, pound(s) — An adverb;
  lit. (pounds) in weight.
stateram (acc.), scales
pondus eris n, weight

67c

capsellam (acc.), locket
*aureolus a um, little gold(en) —
  Dim. of *aureus.
Felicionem (acc.), Luck Lad
crotalium ī n, earring

in vicem, in her turn
excatarissasti me, you cleaned
  me out
faba ae f, bean
*auricula ae f, little ear — Dim.
  of *auris.
praeciderem, I'd cut off
pro luto, dirt-cheap

67d

sauciae (nom.), tipsy — Lit.
  wounded.
junxerunt oscula, joined, i.e.
  added, one kiss to another
  repeatedly — An indication of
  their inebriation.
diligentiam . . . jactat, ranted on
  and on about her own atten-
  tiveness to her matronly duties
delicias . . . viri, (about) her
  husband's pet slave and his
  inattentiveness to her

96

sic cohaerent, Habinnas furtim consurrexit, pedesque
Fortunatae correptos super lectum immisit. "Au, au!"
illa proclamavit, aberrante tunica super genua. Composita
ergo in gremio Scintillae incensissimam rubore faciem
sudario abdidit.

Interposito deinde spatio, cum SECUNDAS MENSAS   68a
Trimalchio jussisset afFERRI, sustulerunt servi omnes
mensas et alias attulerunt, scobemque croco et minio
tinctam sparserunt. Statim Trimalchio, "Poteram quidem,"
inquit, "hoc FERIculo esse contentus; SECUNDAS enim
MENSAS habetis. . . . Sed si quid belli habes, afFER."

---

cohaerent, were engrossing each
other — Find English deriva-
tives and cognates for this and
other words in this passage.
furtim, secretly — i.e. without the
women realizing it.
*cōnsurgō ere surrēxī surrēctus
(con + *surgō), rise up, get up
(from table)
pedesque — Instead of sitting at
table, like women of the old
school, Fortunata and Scintilla
are reclining like men (Cp.
discumbebat, 67a), with their
feet over the back edge of the
couch (Cp. on *pedes*, 58a).
genua (acc.), her knees
gremio (abl.), bosom
incensissimam rubore, blushing
as red as fire
sudario, in her handkerchief

68a

SECUNDAS MENSAS — En
garde! To the guests, the
words *secundas mensas* mean
dessert, but the waiters take
them literally.
scobemque . . . tinctam (acc.),
sawdust colored with saffron
and vermilion — To hide the
wine stains on the floor as

sand was used to cover blood
in the amphitheater!
hoc FERIculo — i.e. the empty
tables! *Ferculum* means a
course of food but is derived
from *fero*, bring; the *bringing*
of the tables is therefore a
ferculum. Trimalchio under-
scores his point by using, and
of course distorting, the vulgar
pronunciation *fericulum*, to
echo *afferi*.
afFER, fetch it in — The singular
imperative shows that this
sentence is addressed to the
butler, doubtless after an impressive pause. Note the
egotism of such elaborate
staging for a practical joke
and a double-edged pun. Almost as brainless as: "Please
serve the dessert." Empty
plates served with a flourish.
General consternation.
"What's wrong? You've got
your deserts, at least all that
was de-served." Butler looks
sheepish. "Oh well, serve
'em *right*! Give 'em *more*'n
they D-serve." — Big joke!
No? Trimalchio thought so,
but Petronius thought the joke
was on Trimalchio.

97

Interim puer Alexandrinus qui caldam ministrabat,   68b
luscinias coepit imitari, clamante Trimalchione subinde,
"Muta!"
Ecce alius ludus. Servus qui ad pedes Habinnae
sedebat, jussus, credo, a domino suo, proclamavit subito
canora voce:

"Intereá medium Aéneás jam clásse tenébat . . ."

Nullus sonus umquam acidior percussit aures meas, ut
tunc primum me etiam Vergilius offenderit.

Plausum tamen, cum tandem destitisset, adjecit   68c
Habinnas et, "Numquam," inquit, "didicit, sed ego ad
circulatores eum mittendo docebam. Itaque parem non
habet, sive muliones volet sive circulatores imitari.
Desperatum valde ingeniosus est: idem sutor est, idem
cocus, idem pistor, omnis musae puer. Duo tamen vitia
habet, quae si non haberet, esset omnium numerum:
recutitus est et stertit. Nam quod strabonus est, non curo.
Sicut Venus spectat. Ideo nihil tacet, vix oculo mortuo
umquam. Illum emi trecentis denariis."

68b

caldam ministrabat, served hot
  water — Used to warm the wine.
luscinias (acc.), bird calls — Lit.
  nightingales.
ludus ī m, skit, stunt
canora (abl.), sing-song
Aeneas (nom.) — Aeneas, hero of
  Vergil's *Aeneid,* part of which
  the boy now starts to recite.

68c

ad circulatores, to hawkers —
  Street vendors boomed out
  their wares, which were borne
  by mules.
muliones (acc.), mule drivers
desperatum, desperately, awfully
sutor, a shoemaker

pistor, a baker
musa ae f, ability — Lit. muse,
  goddess of inspiration.
vitia (acc.), defects
omnium numer(or)um, tiptop —
  Lit. of all counts, i.e. of the
  greatest account.
recutitus . . . stertit, he is cir-
  cumcised and he snores
quod strabonus est, as for the
  fact that he flutters his eyes
  — Lit. he is cross-eyed.
  Editors have almost become
  cross-eyed themselves trying
  to see some sense in this
  passage. Obviously the boy,
  like Venus, goddess of love,
  has that come-hither look in
  his eyes — or at least
  Habinnas thinks so.

Interpellavit loquentem Scintilla et, "Plane," inquit,   69a
"non omnia artificia servi nequam narras. Agaga est.
At curabo, stigmam habeat."
    Risit Trimalchio et, "Adcognosco," inquit, "Cappa-
docem. Nihil sibi defraudit, et mehercules laudo illum.
Hoc enim nemo parentat. Tu autem, Scintilla, noli zelotypa
esse. Crede mihi, et vos novimus. Sic me salvum habeatis,
ut ego sic solebam dominam meam debattuere ut etiam
dominus suspicaretur. Et ideo me in vilicationem
relegavit. Sed tace, lingua; dabo panem."
    Tamquam laudatus esset, nequissimus servus lucernam 69b
de sinu fictilem protulit, et amplius semihora tubicines

69a

Interpellavit, interrupted
nequam (indeclinable), good for
    nothing
Agaga, a pimp
(ut) stigmam habeat, that he
    gets branded for it — Branding
    was sometimes used as a
    punishment; even among slaves
    it was regarded as a disgrace.
    Cp. 45c, and study "stigma"
    in your English dictionary.
Adcognosco Cappadocem, I have
    a fellow feeling for such a
    Cappadocian — i.e. an ag-
    gressive, enterprising fellow
    like Trimalchio himself.
defraudit, denies — Literally?
Hoc enim nemo parentat, Sex is
    one thing you can't take with
    you, and that's for sure. — Lit.
    No one makes an offering to
    the dead with this. The
    Parentalia was a festival at
    which offerings were made to
    the dead (parentare), who were
    thus provided with wine, milk,
    honey, oil, and the blood of
    black victims, but as Trimal-
    chio says, nothing by way of
    sex!

zelotypa, jealous
vos, you (women) — Women have
    their affairs, too, as Trimal-
    chio can testify from experi-
    ence.
Sic — ut, As (I hope that) . . .
    (I swear) that . . .
debattuere, to make love to —
    Lit. to beat up. Cp. French
    débattre.
in vilicationem, to the manage-
    ment of a country estate
    (villa)

69b

nequissimus (nom.), utterly
    worthless
fictilis e, made of clay
tubicines (acc.), trumpeters —
    Clay lamps had somewhat the
    same shape as sweet potatoes.
    Since they had two or more
    holes in them, you might
    (after several martinis) mis-
    take one for some kind of
    musical instrument, e.g. an
    ocarina, but you would have to
    stretch both your imagination
    and the lamp to make it
    resemble a trumpet.

imitatus est, succinente Habinna et inferius labrum manu deprimente. Denique vocatum ad se Habinnas basiavit, potionemque illi dedit et, "Tanto melior," inquit, "Massa; dono tibi caligas."

Nec ullus tot malorum finis fuisset, nisi epidipnis   69c esset allata, turdi siliginei uvis passis nucibusque farsi. Insecuta sunt Cydonia etiam mala spinis confixa, ut echinos efficerent. Et haec quidem tolerabilia erant, si non ferculum longe monstrosius effecisset ut vel fame perire mallemus. Nam cum positus esset, ut nos putabamus, anser altilis circaque pisces et omnia genera avium, "Amici," inquit Trimalchio, "quicquid videtis hic positum, de uno corpore est factum."

Ego, scilicet homo prudentissimus, statim intellexi   69d quid esset, et respiciens Agamemnonem, "Mirabor," inquam, "nisi omnia ista de fimo facta sunt aut certe de luto. Vidi Romae Saturnalibus ejusmodi cenarum imaginem fieri."

Nondum finieram sermonem, cum Trimalchio ait, "Ita   70a crescam patrimonio, non corpore, ut ista cocus meus de porco fecit. Non potest esse pretiosior homo. Et ideo

---

succinente Habinna (abl. abs.), with Habinnas whistling an accompaniment
manu — For the effect, try whistling this way yourself.
dono tibi caligas, I'll give you (a new pair of) shoes

69c

epidipnis (nom.), dessert
turdi . . . farsi, thrush-shaped wheat cakes stuffed with raisins and nuts
Cydonia . . . efficerent, quinces studded with thorns to resemble sea-urchins

anser altilis (mas.), a well-fattened goose
avium, of game birds

69d

fimo (abl.), dung
luto (abl.), clay
Saturnalibus, at the Saturnalia — See on *Io Saturnalia*, 58a.
imaginem (acc.), imitation — Cp. rubber wieners served as hot dogs.

70a

Ita — ut — See on *Sic — ut*, 69a.
pretiosus a um, valuable

100

ingenio meo impositum est illi nomen bellissimum; nam
Daedalus vocatur. Et quia bonam mentem habet, attuli
illi Roma munus, cultros Norico ferro." Quos statim
jussit afferri, ut mucronem ad buccam probaremus.

Jam coeperat Fortunata velle saltare, jam Scintilla   70b
frequentius plaudebat quam loquebatur, cum Trimalchio,
"Permitto," inquit, "Philargyre et Cario, etsi
prasinianus es famosus; dic et Menophilae, contubernali tuae, discumbat."

Quid multa? Paene de lectis dejecti sumus, adeo   70c
totum triclinium familia occupaverat. Certe ego notavi
super me positum cocum, qui de porco anserem fecerat,
muria condimentisque fetentem. Nec contentus fuit
discumbere, sed continuo Ephesum tragoedum coepit
imitari et subinde dominum suum sponsione provocare
"si prasinus proximis circensibus primam palmam."

---

ingenium ī n, ingenuity
Daedalus — Famous craftsman
  of Cretan mythology, but his
  name had become proverbial
  for Jack of all trades.
cultros (acc.), (a set of) knives
Norico (abl.), Noric — i.e. fine,
  excellent.
mucronem (acc.), edge, sharp-
  ness
ad buccam, on our cheeks —
  Ouch! This does *not* refer to
  shaving. Note how Trimalchio
  just has to show off the most
  recently acquired household
  gadget.

70b

saltare, to dance
Permitto = Permitto (ut) discum-
  batis
Philargyre et Cario (voc.) — Two
  of the household slaves.
prasinianus (nom.), a Green fan
  — Charioteers who drove
  horses in the circus races

were furnished by four syndi-
cates, whose drivers were
distinguished by the colors
they wore: red, white, blue,
and green. In Imperial times
these races were very popular,
betting was widespread, and
free-for-all fights frequently
took place between supporters
of different colors.
contubernali — See on *contuber-*
nalis, 57b.

70c

Quid multa? = Quid multa dicam?
anserem (acc.), a goose
muria . . . fetentem, stinking of
  pickles and sauces — With
  cocum.
Ephesum tragoedum (acc.), the
  tragic actor Ephesus — Whoever *he* was!
sponsione (abl.), with a bet
si prasinus . . . palmam, that a
  Green would win first place at
  the next races.

Diffusus hac contentione Trimalchio, "Amici," 71a
inquit, "et servi homines sunt et aeque unum lactem
biberunt, etiam si illos malus fatus oppressit. Tamen
me salvo, cito aquam liberam gustabunt. Ad summam,
omnes illos in testamento meo manu mitto. Nam
Fortunatam meam heredem facio, et commendo illam
omnibus amicis meis. Et haec ideo omnia publico, ut
familia mea jam nunc sic me amet tamquam mortuum."

Gratias agere omnes indulgentiae coeperant domini, 71b
cum ille oblitus nugarum, exemplar testamenti jussit
afferri et totum a primo ad ultimum, ingemescente familia,
recitavit. Respiciens deinde Habinnam, "Quid dicis,"
inquit, "amice carissime? Aedificas monumentum meum
quemadmodum te jussi? Valde te rogo ut secundum pedes
statuae meae catellam ponas et coronas et unguenta et
Petraitis omnes pugnas, ut mihi contingat tuo beneficio
post mortem vivere; praeterea ut sint in fronte pedes
centum, in agrum pedes ducenti. Omne genus enim

71a

Diffusus (nom.), softened, ex-
    pansive — From *diffundo;* cp.
    perfundo.
Aeque . . . biberunt, they drunk
    their mother's milk, just as we
    did — With somewhat the same
    effect as people say drunk for
    drank, Trimalchio says
    lactem (m.) for *lac* (n.), milk;
    in the very next clause he
    also says *fatus* (m.) for
    fatum (n.).
testamentum i n, will — He has
    just promised the slaves their
    freedom if he lives *(me salvo);*
    now they will get their free-
    dom if he dies! His thinking
    is as confused as his genders.
manu mitto — See on *manu misit,*
    42c.
heres edis m or f, heir
publicare, to let (something) be
    known

71b

nugarum (gen.), trivialities —
    Trimalchio now becomes very
    serious.
exemplar (acc.), a copy
ingemescente (abl.), moaning
    and groaning
*aedificō āre āvī ātus, build,
    construct
catellam (acc.), my li'l dog —
    Described in 64b as *canis
    ingentis formae.*
Petraitis, of Petraites —
    Trimalchio's favorite gladi-
    ator; cp. 52a.
in fronte, frontage — i.e. the ex-
    tent of the burial plot along
    the road. See on *monumentum,*
    62b.
Omne genus poma, all kinds of
    fruit trees — i.e. plenty of
    them. Whatever the grammar
    or usage may be, this is
    clearly what Trimalchio means.

poma volo sint circa cineres meos, et vinearum largiter.
Valde enim falsum est vivo quidem domos cultas esse,
non curari eas ubi diutius nobis habitandum est. Et
ideo ante amnia adjici volo: 'Hoc monumentum
heredem non sequitur.'
"Ceterum erit mihi curae ut testamento caveam ne   71c
mortuus injuriam accipiam. Praeponam enim unum ex
libertis sepulcro meo, custodiae causa, ne in monumentum meum populus cacatum currat. Te rogo ut naves etiam
in monumento meo facias, plenis velis euntes, et me in
tribunali sedentem, praetextatum cum anulis aureis quinque, et nummos in publico de sacculo effundentem. Scis

---

cineres (acc.), ashes
vinearum largiter, lots 'n' lots
  of grapevines
falsum, wrong
vivo — Dative of possession.
cultus a um, well kept
eas (domos) ubi, the homes in
  which
heredem (acc.), the heir — The
  formula here used is often
  found on ancient tombs (ab-
  breviated H.M.H.N.S.), to ensure their continuing to be
  part of the family property.
  Cp. Friedländer ad loc. In
  this case, since Trimalchio
  has no blood relatives and his
  wife cannot dispose of the
  cemetery property, Trimalchio
  is, in effect, trying to have
  property in his own name after
  he is dead.

71c

ut . . . caveam, to take precau-
  tions in my will

cacatum — Supine of purpose.
  For meaning see on ad stelas
  facere, 62b.
velum ī n, a sail
in tribunali, on a dais —
  Trimalchio, like Habinnas
  (See on Habinnas, 65a), had
  served for a term as a priest
  of the Emperor cult. During
  his tenure of this public office
  (which was of no real political
  importance), he was entitled
  to sit on the platform at public
  functions and to wear the
  purple-bordered toga. On taking office he gave a public
  banquet for the townspeople,
  distributed money to them, and
  on the strength of this, was
  apparently granted, or simply
  assumed, the right to wear
  gold rings. See on eques
  Romanus, 57b.
praetextatum (acc.), wearing a
  purple-bordered toga
anulis (abl.), rings
nummos (acc.), cash
sacculo (abl.), bag

103

enim quod epulum dedi binos denarios. Faciatur, si
tibi videtur, et triclinia. Facias et totum populum sibi
suaviter facientem.

"Ad dextram meam ponas statuam Fortunatae meae, 71d
columbam tenentem. Et catellam cingulo alligatam
ducat. Et cicaronem meum, et amphoras copiosas gypsatas
ne effluant vinum. Et urnam licet fractam sculpas, et
super eam puerum plorantem. Horologium in medio, ut
quisquis horas inspiciet, velit nolit, nomen meum legat.

"Inscriptio quoque vide diligenter si haec satis ido- 71e
nea tibi videtur: 'C. Pompeius Trimalchio Maecenatianus
hic requiescit. Huic seviratus absenti decretus est.
Cum posset in omnibus decuriis Romae esse, tamen noluit.
Pius, fortis, fidelis, ex parvo crevit. Sestertium reliquit
trecenties, nec umquam philosophum audivit. Vale. Et
tu.' "

---

quod dedi = me dedisse — See on
  quod, 46b.
epulum (acc.), a public banquet
Faciatur — Regularly, *fiat.*
  Strictly, Trimalchio should
  have said *fiant,* to go with
  triclinia, which here means
  picnic tables.

  71d

columbam (acc.), a dove
catellam . . . alligatam (acc.), a
  little dog on a leash
cicaronem (acc.), my boy —
  Trimalchio probably means
  Croesus, 64a; from 74d, *non
  patiaris,* etc., we know that he
  had no children.
gypsatus a um, sealed
sculpas, you may carve — Sub-
  junctive, with *ut* implied.
Horologium, a sundial — Supply
  sit.

velit nolit, whether he wants to
  or not — Review *volo* and *nolo.*

  71e

C., Gaius — Not Caius.
requiescit, rests, lies
seviratus (nom.), the sevirate —
  i.e. the office of priest of the
  Emperor cult, which was given
  by decree of the local senate.
decuriis (abl.), branches of the
  civil service
pius a um, dutiful — This is the
  word Vergil uses to describe
  Aeneas as the model of Roman
  morality, dutiful in all things
  human and divine.
Sestertium trecenties, thirty
  million sesterces
Vale. Et tu, Farewell (addressed
  to the passer-by). Farewell to
  you (the supposed reply).

Haec ut dixit Trimalchio, flere coepit ubertim. 72a
Flebat et Fortunata. Flebat et Habinnas. Tota denique
familia, tamquam in funus rogata, lamentatione triclinium
implevit. Immo jam coeperam etiam ego plorare, cum
Trimalchio, "Ergo," inquit, "cum sciamus nos morituros
esse, quare non vivamus? Sic vos felices videam, con-
jiciamus nos in balneum; meo periculo, non paenitebit.
Sic calet tamquam furnus."

"Vero, vero," inquit Habinnas, "de una die duas
facere, nihil malo," nudisque consurrexit pedibus, et
Trimalchionem plaudentem subsequi coepit.

Ego respiciens ad Ascylton, "Quid cogitas?" inquam. 72b
"Ego enim si videro balneum, statim exspirabo."

"Assentemur," ait ille, "et dum illi balneum petunt,
nos in turba exeamus."

Cum haec placuissent, ducente per porticum Gitone,
ad januam venimus, ubi canis catenarius tanto nos
tumultu excepit ut Ascyltos etiam in piscinam ceciderit.
Nec non ego quoque ebrius, qui etiam pictum timueram
canem, dum natanti opem fero, in eundem gurgitem
tractus sum.

72a

ubertim, copiously
funus (acc.), his funeral
Sic — See on *Sic — ut*, 69a.
non paenitebit, it will cause you
    no regrets — Trimalchio thinks
    no harm will come from bathing
    after a heavy meal; if it does,
    he'll take the blame for it.
Sic . . . furnus, It's as hot as an
    oven
de una die duas, two days out of
    one

72b

Ascylton (acc.) — See page 37.

Assentemur, Let's let 'em think
    we agree with 'em.
in turba, in the confusion
porticus ūs f, portico — Here a
    peri-style, a yard containing a
    colonnade, with a door opening
    into the street.
Gitone (abl.) — See page 37.
catenarius (nom.), chained (to
    the doorpost)
piscinam (acc.), fish pool
natanti (dat.), to him as he tried
    to swim (out)
gurgitem (acc.), maelstrom —
    Comic exaggeration, implying
    that the pool is large, deep,
    and all churned up with
    Ascyltos' frantic lashing.

Servavit nos tamen atriensis, qui interventu suo et   72c
canem placavit et nos trementes extraxit in siccum. Et
Giton quidem jam dudum se ratione prudentissima redeme-
rat a cane; quicquid enim a nobis acceperat de cena, latranti sparserat, et ille avocatus cibo, furorem
suppresserat.
Ceterum cum algentes utique petissemus ab atriense
ut nos extra januam emitteret, "Erras," inquit, "si
putas te exire hac posse, qua venisti. Nemo umquam con-
vivarum per eandem januam emissus est. Alia intrant,
alia exeunt."
Quid faciamus, homines miserrimi et novi generis   73a
labyrintho inclusi, quibus lavari jam coeperat votum
esse? Ultro ergo rogamus ut nos ad balneum duceret,
projectisque vestimentis, quae Giton in aditu siccare
coepit, balneum intravimus, ubi Trimalchio in aqua
rectus stabat.
Ac ne sic quidem putidissimam jactationem licuit   73b
effugere. Nam nihil melius esse dicebat quam sine
turba lavari, et eo ipso loco aliquando pistrinum fuisse.
Deinde ut lassatus consedit, invitatus balnei sono,

72c

atriensis (nom.), the major-domo
placavit, quieted
trementes (acc.), shivering
in siccum, onto dry land
latranti (dat.), for (the dog as it
  came) barking (at him)
algentes, (since we were)
  chilled (to the bone)
hac, qua, alia, alia — With each
  of these words supply *via*
  (abl.).

73a

labyrintho inclusi, imprisoned in
  a labyrinth
votum (pred. acc.), a good idea —
  The bath would warm them up.

siccare, to dry — Presumably by
  flipping them about in the air.
rectus, bolt upright

73b

putidissimam jactationem (acc.),
  his utterly disgusting exhibi-
  tionism
turba (abl.), a mob of people
  milling about — As would be
  the case in the public baths.
  Trimalchio is pluming himself
  on his having his own private
  bath.
aliquando, at one time
pistrinum (acc.), a bakery
lassatus, he got tired (and)

diduxit usque ad cameram os ebrium, et coepit Menecratis cantica lacerare, sicut illi dicebant qui linguam
ejus intellegebant.
    Ergo ebrietate discussa, e balneo in aliud triclinium
deducti sumus. Tum Trimalchio, "Amici," inquit,
"hodie servus meus barbatoriam fecit, homo praefiscini
frugi et micarius. Itaque tangomenas faciamus, et usque
in lucem cenemus."
    Haec dicente eo, gallus gallinaceus cantavit. Qua   74a
voce confusus, Trimalchio vinum sub mensa jussit
effundi lucernamque etiam mero spargi. Immo anulum
trajecit in dextram manum et, "Non sine causa," inquit
"hic bucinus signum dedit. Nam aut incendium oportet
fiat, aut aliquis in vicinia animam abjiciet. Longe a
nobis! Itaque quisquis hunc indicem attulerit, corollarium accipiet." Dicto citius de vicinia gallus allatus
est, quem Trimalchio occidi jussit, ut aeno coctus
fieret.

---

cameram (acc.), roof
Menecratis, of Menecrates — A
    musician who received a
    special award from the Em-
    peror Nero.
*ēbrietās tātis f, intoxication
    (Cp. *ēbrius)
discussa (abl.), dispelled
barbatoriam fecit, is celebrating
    his first shave — The first
    shave was an occasion for
    festivity; Trimalchio makes
    this an excuse for prolonging
    his own party.
homo . . . micarius, a worthy
    fellow — Touch wood! — and
    thrifty, too
tangomenas, a night of it

74a

gallus gallinaceus (nom.), a
    domestic cock, a rooster

confusus (nom.), flabbergasted —
    Despite Trimalchio's saying
    praefiscini (Touch wood!),
    which was supposed to avert
    evil, the rooster crows, an-
    nouncing "daylight" at the
    very moment he says lucem.
    Such a coincidence is in itself
    a bad omen, but especially so
    since birds and their calls,
    especially that of the rooster,
    were held to be prophetic.
    Hence elaborate precautions
    must now be taken against
    such a bad omen.
mero, with undiluted wine
anulum (acc.), his ring
bucinus (nom.), trumpet player
vicinia ae f, neighborhood
indicem (acc.), prophet
corollarium (acc.), a reward
ut . . . fieret, and to be stewed
    in a saucepan.

Deinde respiciens ad familiam Trimalchio, "Quid vos," inquit, "adhuc non cenastis? Abite, ut alii veniant ad officium." Subiit igitur alia classis, et illi quidem exclamavere, "Vale, Gai!" – hi autem, "Ave, Gai!"

Hinc primum hilaritas nostra turbata est. Nam cum puer non inspeciosus inter novos intrasset ministros, invasit eum Trimalchio et osculari diutius coepit. Itaque Fortunata, ut ex aequo jus firmum approbaret, male dicere Trimalchioni coepit et purgamentum dedecusque praedicare, qui non contineret libidinem suam. Ultimo etiam adjecit, "Canis!" Trimalchio contra offensus convicio calicem in faciem Fortunatae immisit.

Illa tamquam oculum perdidisset, exclamavit manusque trementes ad faciem suam admovit. Conterrita est etiam Scintilla, trepidantemque sinu suo texit. Immo puer quoque officiosus urceolum frigidum ad malam ejus admovit, super quem incumbens Fortunata plorare ac flere coepit.

Contra Trimalchio, "Quid enim?" inquit; "Ambubaia 74c non meminit? Sed de machina illam sustuli; hominem inter homines feci. At inflat se tamquam rana, et in

---

74b

Vale, Farewell
Ave, Hail — But context, assonance and usage suggest: 'Bye, Boss! – Hi, Boss!'
turbata est, was turned into confusion
non inspeciosus (nom.), rather good looking
minister trī m, waiter
invasit, grabbed hold of
ut ex aequo . . . approbaret, to prove her claim upon him equally well founded
purgamentum . . . praedicare, to call him scum and monster

libido dinis f, passion, lust
convicium ī n, insult
calicem (acc.), a cup
trementes (acc. pl.), trembling
trepidantem (acc.), the quivering Fortunata
urceolum frigidum (acc.), a cool water jug
malam (acc.), her cheek

74c

ambubaia (nom.), this jazz artist
machina (abl.), the slave block
inflat, puffs . . . up
rana, a frog — Fable of the frog and the ox.

sinum suum non spuit – codex, non mulier. Sed hic qui
in pergula natus est aedes non somniatur. Ita genium
meum propitium habeam, curabo, domata sit Cassandra
caligaria. "Et ego, homo dipundiarius, sestertium centies   74d
accipere potui. Scis tu me non mentiri. Agatho, un-
guentarius herae proximae, eduxit me et, 'Suadeo,'
inquit, 'non patiaris genus tuum interire.' At ego dum
bonatus ago et nolo videri levis, ipse mihi asciam in
crus impegi. Recte curabo, me unguibus quaeras. Et
ut depraesentiarum intelligas quid tibi feceris, Habinna,
nolo statuam ejus in monumento meo ponas, ne mortuus

---

spuit, spits – To spit in one's
lap was a charm against the
evil eye. Fortunata is so high
and mighty that she thinks no
harm can touch her.
codex, a block(head)
Sed hic qui . . . somniatur, But a
person who's born in the back
shed don't even dream (somniatur should be somniat)
there's a house – As the shed
depends upon the house, so
Fortunata, without admitting
it, depends upon Trimalchio.
Ita = sic as used in 69a, where
see note.
propitius a um, propitious, well
disposed
domata . . . caligaria, that this
theatrical know-it-all gits
(domata should be domita) put
in her place – Cassandra
caligaria is a neat bit of
rhythmical assonance that
must have tickled Trimalchio,
but it has puzzled the com-
mentators no end. Caliga is a
soldier's boot, but Trimalchio
seems to have confused it
with cothurnus, the high shoe
worn by tragic actors.
Cassandra is portrayed in

tragedy as clairvoyant, know-
ing everything by sheer in-
tuition.

74d

homo dipundiarius, penny-wise
fool that I was
sestertium centies, ten million
sesterces
Agatho . . . proximae, Agatho,
the perfumer who supplies the
lady next door – The lady, it
seems, has money and would
be glad to marry Trimalchio
and give him both wealth and
children.
non = ne
bonatus ago, play the good
husband
ipse . . . impegi, I drove the axe
into my own leg – Instead of
"giving" Fortunata the axe,
i.e. divorcing her.
Recte, O.K.!, All right then!
(ut) me unguibus quaeras, that
you will try to dig me out of
my grave with your bare hands
– Lit. seek me with your
finger nails
depraesentiarum, this very minute – Lit. spot cash.

109

quidem lites habeam. Immo, ut sciat me posse malum
dare, nolo me mortuum basiet."

Post hoc fulmen Habinnas rogare coepit ut jam   75a
desineret irasci et, "Nemo," inquit, "nostrum non
peccat. Homines sumus, non dei." Idem et Scintilla
flens dixit ac per genium ejus, Gaium appellando, rogare
coepit ut se frangeret.

Non tenuit diutius lacrimas Trimalchio et, "Rogo,"
inquit, "Habinna, sic peculium tuum fruniscaris, si
quid perperam feci, in faciem meam inspue. Puerum
basiavi frugalissimum, non propter formam, sed quia
frugi est. Decem partes dicit, librum ab oculo legit,
thraecium sibi de diariis fecit, arcisellium de suo
paravit et duas trullas. Non est dignus quem in
oculis feram?

"Sed Fortunata vetat. Ita tibi videtur, fulcipedia?   75b

---

quidem, even — With *mortuus*,
  not with *ne*.
lites (acc.), squabbling,
  nagging

75a

fulmen inis n, thunderbolt
desinere (+ infin.), to stop (doing
  something)
non peccat, makes no mistakes
se frangere, to cool off — Literally?
lacrimas (acc.), tears
sic . . . fruniscaris, by my hope
  that you may enjoy your
  money — Cp. on *Sic — ut*, 69a.
perperam, amiss, wrong
inspue (imperat.), spit
frugalissimum, who has good
  stuff in him
frugi (pred.), a good egg —
  Dative of *frux*, fruit, regularly
  used for *frugalis*, which de-
  notes not merely thrift, but
  sound qualities in general.

Decem . . . dicit, knows his ten
  times table — Cp. on *partes*,
  46b, and on *partes centum*,
  58c.
thraecium . . . fecit, he has acquired a Thracian gladiator's
  outfit out of his daily allow-
  ance — Like a modern young-
  ster who saves up to buy
  himself a cowboy suit. But
  this interpretation is mere
  guess work and seems highly
  unlikely in view of the probable age of the boy and the
  other acquisitions listed
  below.
arcisellium (acc.), a round-
  backed chair
trullas (acc.), ladles
in oculis — Cp. Engl. the apple
  of one's eye.

75b

vetat, forbids (it)
fulcipedia, you high-heeled prima
  donna

Suadeo, bonum tuum concoquas, milva, et me non facias
ringentem, amasiuncula; alioquin experieris cerebrum
meum. Nosti me; quod semel destinavi, clavo tabulari
fixum est.
"Sed vivorum meminerimus. Vos rogo, amici, ut   75c
vobis suaviter sit. Nam ego quoque tam fui quam vos
estis, sed virtute mea ad hoc perveni. Corcillum est
quod homines facit, cetera quisquilia omnia. 'Bene
emo, bene vendo'; alius alia vobis dicet. Felicitate
dissilio. Tu autem, sterteia, etiam nun ploras? Jam
curabo, fatum tuum plores.
"Sed ut coeperam dicere, ad hanc me fortunam
frugalitas mea perduxit. Tam magnus ex Asia veni quam
hic candelabrus est. Ad summam, cotidie me solebam
ad illum metiri, et ut celerius rostrum barbatum haberem,
labra de lucerna ungebam.

---

bonum tuum concoquas, milva, to
 reflect upon your good luck,
 you vulture — More guess work.
 Cp. edd.
ringentem, show my teeth
amasiuncula, my sweet little
 lovey-dovey
alioquin, otherwise
cerebrum meum, how mad I can
 get — Lit. my brain.
destinavi, I have settled
clavo tabulari, with a spike

75c

meminerimus — See on *meminī,
 43a.
corcillum i n, a little brain work
quisquilia (neut. pl.), just odds
 and ends, rubbish
*fēlīcitās tātis f (cp. *fēlīciter),

happiness, prosperity
dissilio, I'm just exploding
sterteia, you sniveler
frugalitas mea (nom.), my own
 merit, ability, competence —
 See on *frugi, 75a.
hic candelabrus (nom.), this here
 lamp stand — Trimalchio
 should have said *hoc
 candelabrum* (neut.).
metiri, to measure
rostrum barbatum, a beard on my
 beak
ungebam, I used to smear — Apparently the boy Trimalchio
 thought that oil from
 candelabra would be good for
 his own *labra*, as if *candelabrus*, as he calls it, were
 derived from *candeo*, be bright
 or attractive, and *labrum*, lip!

Written Exercise 64-75

1 (ōsculātī, 64a) The ancients were accustomed to kiss the table
 for (so that they might have) good luck. We ought not to laugh at
 them. We do not kiss the table, but we do "touch wood"

111

(lignum ī n.). The word *ōsculum* means *(significō āre)* ‶little mouth.″ What does *ōsculor* mean?

2 *(lucernae,* 64a) Our friend said that it seemed to him that more lamps were burning in the dining room. He must have been drunk, because there really were no more lamps.

3 *(bāsiāvit,* 64d) If the words *bāsiāre* and *ōsculārī* mean the same (thing), what does *perbāsiāre* mean?

4 *(assurgere,* 65a; *cōnsurrēxit,* 67d) We have seen and read the words *surgere, assurgere,* and *cōnsurgere.* Do you think that all these words ought to mean the same (thing)?

5 *(plaudentem,* 67a) I know that the guests are all applauding, because with my own ears I hear them applauding, but I do not know to whom they are giving their applause.

6 *(aureolam,* 67c) If you know the word *aurum,* it is not difficult to learn *aureus,* and if you knew the word *aureus,* you would easily learn *aureolus.*

7 *(auriculās,* 67c) If you had learned the word *auris,* you would have found it easy to guess *(conjectāre)* what *auricula* meant.

8 *(aedificās,* 71b) He ordered his tomb to be built because he believed that he was going to die, but his friend was unwilling to build the tomb because he did not believe that he was going to die.

9 *(ēbrietāte,* 73b; *fēlīcitāte,* 75c) You don't think that drunkenness and happiness are the same (thing, do you)? To a drunk (man) it seems so because he thinks himself happy. Good luck to all, both drunk and happy!

"Ceterum, quemadmodum dei volunt, dominus in domo   76a
factus sum, et ecce cepi ipsimi cerebellum. Quid multa?
Coheredem me Caesari fecit, et accepi patrimonium
laticlavium. Nemini tamen nihil satis est. Concupivi
negotiari. Ne multis vos morer, quinque naves aedificavi,
oneravi vinum (et tunc erat contra aurum), misi Romam.
Putares me hoc jussisse: omnes naves naufragarunt –

76a

ipsimi cerebellum, my master's
  fancy – Lit. the boss's little
  old brain
Quid multa? = *Quid multa dicam?*
Coheredem (acc.) Caesari, coheir
  with the Emperor – Rich men
  commonly left part of their
  estate to the Emperor, to
  avoid outright confiscation.

laticlavium, fit for a senator
negotiari, to be a businessman
contra, worth its weight in
naufragarunt, were shipwrecked
  – Note the word play: All my
  shipping was shipped – *to* the
  bottom! The shipwreck was
  so much like clockwork you
  would have thought the
  shipper planned it that way.

factum, non fabula. Uno die Neptunus trecenties
sestertium devoravit.

"Putatis me defecisse? Non mehercules mi haec   76b
jactura gusti fuit — tamquam nihil facti. Alteras naves
feci majores et meliores et feliciores, ut nemo non me
virum fortem diceret. Scitis, magna navis magnam
fortitudinem habet. Oneravi rursus vinum, lardum,
fabam, seplasium, mancipia. Hoc loco Fortunata rem
piam fecit. Omne enim aurum suum, omnia vestimenta
vendidit et mi centum aureos in manu posuit. Hoc
fuit peculii mei fermentum. Cito fit quod dei volunt.
Uno cursu centies sestertium corrotundavi.

"Statim redemi fundos omnes, qui patroni mei fuerant.   76c
Aedifico domum. Venalicia coemo — jumenta. Quicquid
tangebam crescebat tamquam favus. Postquam coepi
plus habere quam tota patria mea habet, manum de tabula:
sustuli me de negotiatione et coepi libertos faenerare.

---

fabula — Reproduce the allitera-
  tion in your English.
Neptunus, Neptune, god of the
  sea
trecenties sestertium, thirty
  million sesterces

76b

defecisse, gave in
jactura ae f, loss
gusti, even a flea bite — Lit.
  worth a taste. *Gusti* is gen.
  of value.
magna navis — To Trimalchio a
  big ship is a symbol of himself.
lardum . . . mancipia, bacon,
  beans, perfume, and slaves
pius a um, noble — See on *pius,*
  71e.
peculii mei fermentum, my nest
  egg — Lit. the leaven of my
  savings.
centies . . . corrotundavi, I made

a profit of ten million sesterces — Lit. rounded up.

76c

fundus ī m, estate
Venalicia . . . jumenta, I bought
  up slaves — horses and mules,
  I mean — The word play defies
  grammar. *Venalicia* starts out
  as a noun meaning *slaves,* but
  ends up as an adjective modi-
  fying *jumenta,* draught animals
  to sell.
favus ī m, honeycomb
manum de tabula, I let well
  enough alone — Proverbial.
  Lit. (I took) my hand away
  from the picture (like a
  painter who knows when to
  stop retouching).
de negotiatione, from commercial
  activity
faenerare, to finance — Like the
  aristocrats, he loaned money
  to freedmen at interest and let
  them take the risks of com-
  merce.

"Et sane nolentem me negotium meum agere exhortavit 76d
mathematicus, qui venerat forte in coloniam nostram,
Graeculio, Serapa nomine, consiliator deorum. Hic mihi
dixit etiam ea quae oblitus eram. Ab acia et acu mi
omnia exposuit. Intestinas meas noverat. Tantum quod
mihi non dixerat, quid pridie cenaveram. Putasses
illum semper mecum habitasse.

"Rogo, Habinna — puto, interfuisti —: 'Tu dominam   77a
tuam de rebus illis fecisti. Tu parum felix in amicos es.

76d

sane, me, meum — Emphatic,
comparing his own hesitant
start in business with that of
the freedmen just mentioned.

exhortavit — Deponentitis
again!

mathematicus ī m, a fortune
teller

Graeculio (nom.), a little Greek
guy

consiliator, counselor, con-
sultant — He could have told
the gods themselves a thing
or two

Ab acia et acu, down to the
darnedest detail — Lit. from
thread and needle, proverbial
for small details. Cp. Needles
and pins, needles and pins!
When a man marries, his
trouble begins.

Tantum, (There was) only one
thing

77a

interfuisti, you were there
(when the fortune teller said
to me . . .) — Trimalchio pro-
ceeds to mimic the fortune
teller, impressively quoting
the actual (?) words.

Tu . . . fecisti, You got your

good wife from you know
where — Lit. you made the
respectable mistress of your
house out of the well known
business. *Dominam,* mistress
of a house *(domus),* implies
respectable status. *Rebus
illis = rebus veneriis,* but *illis*
is used suggestively for
veneriis, with the common
meaning of well known.
Fecisti is used as in *hominem
inter homines feci,* 74c. —
This sentence is not merely a
nasty slur on Fortunata. It is
a subtle revelation of Trimalchio's deep sense of failure.
Outwardly, he has won social
status; inwardly he still re-
sents his own background.
His resentment takes various
ugly forms — here, that of
vituperation against his wife,
who symbolizes his background,
because she is a constant reminder of the fact that he
could not have married into
respectable society if he
wanted to. He can not respect
her because he does not respect himself. — The present
passage is only one of many
in which Petronius shows himself a great artist and a sound
psychologist.

parum, not very

Nemo umquam tibi parem gratiam refert. Tu latifundia possides. Tu viperam sub ala nutricas.' Et – quid vobis non dixerim et nunc mi restare vitae annos triginta et menses quattuor et dies duos?

"Praeterea cito accipiam hereditatem. Hoc mihi dicit   77b
fatus meus. Quod si contigerit fundos Apuliae jungere, satis vivus pervenero. Interim dum Mercurius vigilat, aedificavi hanc domum. Ut scitis, casula erat. Nunc templum est. Habet quattuor triclinia, cubicula viginti, porticus marmoratos duos, susum triclinium, cubiculum in quo ipse dormio, viperae hujus sessorium, ostiarii cellam perbonam. Et multa alia sunt quae statim vobis ostendam. Credite mihi, assem habeas, assem valeas; habes, habeberis. Sic amicus vester, qui fuit rana, nunc est rex.

"Interim, Stiche, profer vitalia in quibus volo me ef-   77c
ferri. Profer et unguentum, et ex illa amphora gustum ex qua jubeo lavari ossa mea."

---

latifundia (acc.), extensive farm lands
Tu viperam . . . nutricas, You are nursing a viper in your bosom
non dixerim (subjc.), shouldn't I tell . . . that . . .?
et nunc, right now
restare, remain

77b

hereditatem (acc.), an inheritance
fatus (= fatum n.), fate, horoscope
fundos . . . jungere, (for me) to unite my estates with Apulia – A mere matter of buying up the whole southeast district of Italy!
vivus: i.e. for one man's lifetime
Mercurius – See on caduceum, 29b.
casula erat, it (the original building) was a mere shack
cubiculum ī n, bedroom

porticus marmoratos, marble porticoes – Cp. on porticus, 72b.
susum, upstairs
dormio, I sleep
viperae . . . sessorium, this viper's boudoir
ostiarii . . . perbonam, an excellent butler's pantry – Well stocked with silverware; see 37c.
habes, habeberis, make profit, become a prophet – Literally? See vocabulary.
rana ae f, a frog

77c

Stiche (voc.), Stichus – One of the slaves.
vitalia ium n, grave clothes
efferi (= ex + ferri), to be buried – Literally?
gustum, a taste, a drop
ossa (acc.), bones, i.e. dead body – Cp. 65c.

Non est moratus Stichus, sed et stragulam albam et   78a
praetextam in triclinium attulit, jussitque Trimalchio
nos temptare an bonis lanis essent confectae. Tum
subridens, "Vide tu," inquit, "Stiche, ne ista mures
tangant aut tineae. Alioquin te vivum comburam. Ego
gloriosus volo efferri, ut totus mihi populus bene
imprecetur."

Statim ampullam nardi aperuit, omnesque nos unxit   78b
et, "Spero," inquit, "futurum ut aeque me mortuum juvet
tamquam vivum." Nam vinum quidem in vinarium jussit
infundi et, "Putate vos," ait, "ad parentalia mea in-
vitatos esse."

Ibat res ad summam nauseam, cum Trimalchio,
ebrietate turpissima gravis, cornicines in triclinium jussit
adduci, fultusque cervicalibus multis, extendit se super
torum extremum et, "Fingite me," inquit, "mortuum
esse. Dicite aliquid belli."

78a

stragula ae f, a winding sheet
praetextam (acc.), a purple-
    bordered toga — Which, as
    priest of the Emperor cult,
    Trimalchio had once been
    entitled to wear.
subridens, with a wry smile —
    Literally?
tineae (nom.), moths
alioquin, otherwise
comburam, I will burn
efferri, to be buried
bene imprecetur, may call down
    blessings

78b

ampullam (acc.) nardi, the bottle
    of nard — A very expensive oil
    used as perfume.
unxit, anointed
vinarium (acc.), a wine bowl —

Used as we use a punch bowl
to serve from. The party is
about to start all over again!
parentalia ium, funeral feast
cornicines (acc.), trumpeters
fultusque . . . multis, propped up
    with a multitude of cushions
extremum, from end to end of it
    — Instead of lying on his side
    obliquely across the couch, as
    was usual when dining, he lies
    like a corpse on a bier, full
    length, flat on his back and
    raised up high. Friedländer
    and Sedgwick take *torum ex-*
    tremum to mean the edge of
    the couch, but it is just as
    hard to parallel this use of
    extremum as the one given
    above. Petronius did not need
    to specify both ends of the
    couch because normally
    neither end, strictly speaking,
    was occupied.
Fingite (imperat.), Pretend

116

Consonuere cornicines funebri strepitu. Unus
praecipue servus tam valde intonuit ut totam concitaret
viciniam. Itaque vigiles, qui custodiebant viciniam, rati
ardere Trimalchionis domum, effregerunt januam subito,
et cum aqua securibusque tumultari suo jure coeperunt.
Nos occasionem opportunissimam nacti, Agamemnoni
verba dedimus, raptimque tam plane quam ex incendio
fugimus.

78c

Consonuere . . . strepitu, The
  musicians blared out a noisy
  dirge
intonuit, thundered away
concitaret, he aroused
vicinia ae f, neighborhood
vigiles (nom. m. pl.), the fire
brigade
securibus (abl.), axes
tumultuari, to spread confusion
verba, the go by — *Verba dare*
  (+ dat.), to give mere words or
  lip service, comes to mean
  deceive, fool, or take French
  leave of someone.
raptim, with a rush.

VOCABULARY

ā, ab, by, after, from
abdō ere didī ditus, hide
abeō īre īvī or iī itum, go, reach,
    go away, be off
*aberrō āre āvī (ab + *errō),
    wander off, go astray, get out
    of place
abigō ere ēgī āctus (ab + ago),
    drive away
abīte: Review eō īre.
abjiciō ere jēcī jectus (ab +
    jaciō), throw down, throw away
absēns entis, absent
ac, and
accēdō ere cessī cessum, ap-
    proach, go near
accessēre = accesserunt: See
    accēdō.
accipiō ere cēpī ceptus (ad +
    capiō), get, accept, receive
accurrō ere currī or cucurrī cur-
    sus (ad + currō), run up, run to
acidus a um, acid, sour, sharp
ad, to, for, near, at, by, as far
    as, to the accompaniment of
    (music)
addūcō ere dūxī ductus (ad +
    dūcō), bring

adeō, so, to such an extent
*adhūc, still, yet
aditus ūs m, entrance way
adjiciō ere jēcī jectus (ad +
    jaciō), add
adjuvō āre jūvī jūtus (ad + juvō),
    help
admīrātiō ōnis f, admiration,
    amazement
admittō ere mīsī missus (ad +
    mittō), admit
admoneō ēre nuī nitus (ad +
    moneō), remind, warn
admoveō ēre mōvī mōtus (ad +
    moveō), move up, lift up, press
    against
adulēscentulus ī m, young
    fellow
adveniō īre vēnī ventus (ad +
    veniō), come in
adversārius ī m, adversary
adversus, against
*aedificō āre āvī ātus, build,
    construct
aenigma atis n, enigma, riddle
aequē, equally, too, as much
affābilitās tātis f, affability,
    civility

119

afferō afferre attulī allātus (ad + ferō), bring in, take to, import, bring

affīgō ere fīxī fīxus (ad + fīgō), fasten

ager agrī m, field

aggredior ī gressus sum, approach, attack, start in on

agō ere ēgī āctus, celebrate, act, carry on; *agite,* come now!

*ajō ais ait ajunt, etc., assert, say

*albus a um, white

aliēnus a um, not one's own

aliquis aliquī aliqua aliquid aliquod, some, someone, something; any, anyone, anything; a bit of

*aliquot, several, a few

alius a ud, other, another; *alius . . . alius,* one . . . another

allātus: See *afferō.*

alter era erum, other, another, the other, the second; *alter . . . alter,* the one . . . the other

altus a um, high, shrill

*ambulō āre āvī ātus, walk (around)

amīca ae f, girl friend

amīcus ī m, friend

amō āre āvī ātus, like, love

amor ōris m, love

amphitheāter (regularly, *amphitheātrum ī* n), amphitheater

*amphora ae f, wine jar

amplius, more, any more

amplus a um, large

an, whether, or; can it be that . . .?

*anima ae f, breath, soul. See note on *Mihi . . . esse,* 62b.

animadvertō ere tī sus, notice

animus ī m, spirit, mind

annus ī m, year

ante, before, in front of; above (all); sooner, earlier

anteā, formerly

antīquus a um, old, ancient

*aper aprī m, wild boar

aperiō īre uī ertus, open, uncover

apparātus ūs m, apparatus, paraphernalia

appāreō ēre uī itūrus (ad + pāreō), appear, show up, show

appellō āre āvī ātus, call, call by name

appetō ere īvī ītus (ad + petō), go after

approbō āre āvī ātus (ad + probō), prove

apud, with, in, at the house of; *apud quem,* at whose house

aqua ae f, water

*ārdeō ēre ārsī ārsūrus, burn

*argenteus a um, silver, of silver

*argentum ī n, silver

*artificium ī n, trade, profession

*ās assis m, an as; a coin of small value, penny

ascendō ere dī sus, get up

Asia ae f, Asia

*assurgō ere surrēxī surrēctus (ad + *surgō), rise up, get up (from table)

at, but

Athēnae ārum f, Athens

atque, and

attulī: See *afferō.*

audācter, fearlessly

audāculus a um, fearless, courageous

audiō īre īvī ītus, hear, heed, listen to

*auferō auferre abstulī ablātus, remove, take away, carry away

*aureolus a um, little golden

*aureus a um, golden, of gold, gold

*aureus ī m, gold coin

*auricula ae f, little ear

*auris is f, ear

*aurum ī n, gold

aut, or; *aut . . . aut,* either . . . or

autem, however, moreover, but

avidē, avidly, greedily

āvocō āre āvī ātus (ā + vocō), call away, divert

*balneum ī n, bath, bath room
*bāsiō āre āvī ātus, kiss
*belle, neatly, nicely, nice
*bellus a um, nice, pretty
bene, well; *bene esse*, have a
good time; cp. on *suāvis*, 33a.
beneficium ī n, favor, benefit,
kindness
bēstia ae f, beast, animal,
creature
bīnī ae a, two apiece
bis, twice
bonus a um, good
*bōs bovis m, f, ox, bull, cow;
vulgar Latin, *bovis* as
nominative
brevis e, short

cadō ere cecidī cāsūrus, fall
caedō ere cecīdī caesus, cut,
fell, flog, slash at
*caelum ī n, the sky, the
heavens, heaven
canīnus a um, canine
*canis is m, f, dog
*canticum ī n, singing, song
*cantō āre āvī ātus, make music,
sing, play
*capillātus a um, long-haired
capiō ere cēpī captus, capture,
take
caput pitis n, head, person
cārus a um, dear
cāsus ūs m, fall, occurrence
causa ae f, reason; *causā* +
preceding gen., for the sake
of, for the purpose of
ceciderit: Review *cadō*.
celeritās tātis f, speed
celeriter, speedily, quickly
*cēna ae f, dinner, dinner party
*cēnō āre āvī ātus, dine, have
dinner
centum, one hundred
certē, certainly, at least
certus a um, certain, reliable
*cervīx īcis f, neck; plural
frequently used for singular
*cēterum, but, besides
(cēterus) a um, the rest (of)

chorus ī m, chorus, troupe of
singers or dancers
cibus ī m, food
*circā, around
circumeō īre īvī or iī itum, go
around
circumferō ferre tulī lātus, distribute, peddle, carry around
circumlātus: Review *circumfero*.
circumspiciō ere spēxī spectus,
look around
*cito, quickly; comparative,
citius
cīvis is m, citizen
clāmō āre āvī ātus, shout, call
upon
clāmor ōris m, clamor, shouting,
shout
clārus a um, clear, loud
classis is f, fleet, group, shift
cliēns entis m, client; see
Introduction, page 37.
*cocus ī m, a cook
coepī coepisse coeptus, begin
cōgitātiō ōnis f, cogitation,
thought
cōgitō āre āvī ātus, think
cognōscō ere nōvī nitus, learn,
find out; perfect, know
cōgō ere coēgī coāctus, compel
*collībertus ī m, fellow freed-
man; see Introduction page 37.
colligō ere lēgī lēctus, gather up
colloquor ī locūtus sum, con-
verse
*collum ī n, neck
*colōnia ae f, town
color ōris m, color
*comedō ere ēdī ēsus, eat, eat
up
comes itis m, f, companion
commendō āre āvī ātus, com-
mend
compōnō ere posuī positus, put
away, compose, calm
compressus a um, compressed,
restrained
comprobō āre āvī ātus, approve
computō āre āvī ātus, compute,
count up

121

conclāmō āre āvī ātus, shout or
   scream in unison
concupīscō ere cupīvī ītus, long,
   aspire; cp. *cupiō*
concurrō ere currī cursus, run up
cōnficiō ere fēcī fectus (con +
   faciō), make
congerō ere gessī gestus (con +
   gerō), heap up
conjiciō ere jēcī jectus (con +
   jaciō), put into, throw into
conjungō ere jūnxī jūnctus (con
   + jungō), join
cōnor ārī ātus sum, try
cōnsīderō āre āvī ātus, consider
cōnsīdō ere sēdī sessus, sit down
cōnsistō ere stitī stitus, stand,
   come and stand, stand there,
   come to an end
cōnsōlātiō ōnis f, consolation
cōnsūmō ere sūmpsī sūmptus,
   exhaust
*cōnsurgō ere surrēxī surrēctus
   (con + *surgō), rise up, get up
   (from table)
contentiō ōnis f, contention,
   rivalry
contentus a um, content
conterreō ēre uī itus (con +
   terreō), alarm, terrify
contineō ēre uī tentus (con +
   teneō), contain, hold on to,
   restrain
*contingō ere tigī tāctus (con +
   tangō), touch, happen
*continuō, immediately, forthwith
contrā, against, in turn, in reply
convertō ere tī sus (con + vertō),
   turn to
*convīva ae m, f, guest
cōpiōsus a um, copious, large
*corōna ae f, crown, garland
corporāliter, corporeally,
   physically
corpus oris n, body
corrigō ere rēxī rēctus, correct,
   repair
corripiō ere ripuī reptus (con +
   rapiō), seize
cotīdiē, every day

crēdō ere didī ditus, believe
*crēscō ere crēvī crētus, grow,
   grow up, swell, grow rich
cum, with
cum, when, as, since, although
cūra ae f, care, concern
cūrō āre āvī ātus, care, care for,
   look after, see to (it)
currō ere cucurrī cursus, run
cursus ūs m, voyage, trip
custōdia ae f, protection,
   guarding
custōdiō īre īvī ītus, protect,
   guard

dē, down from, concerning, about,
   out of, from, of
dēbeō ēre uī itus, owe, must,
   ought
decem, ten
dēcernō ere crēvī crētus, decree, vote
decimus a um, tenth
dēclāmātiō ōnis f, declamation,
   speech
dēclāmō āre āvī ātus, declaim,
   rehearse
dēdūcō ere dūxī ductus, draw
   away, lure away, take ·
dēferō ferre tulī lātus, take
   down, put down
deinde, then
dējiciō ere jēcī jectus (dē +
   jaciō), throw down, throw out
*dēlectō āre āvī ātus, delight
dēleō ēre ēvī ētus, wipe out,
   destroy
dēlīberō āre āvī ātus, deliberate
dēmittō ere mīsī missus, let down
*dēnārius ī m, denarius; see note
   on 33a.
*dēnique, finally
*dēns dentis m, tooth, tusk
dēpendeō ēre, hang down
dēpōnō ere posuī positus, put
   down
dēprimō ere pressī pressus (dē +
   premō), press down

*dērīdeō ēre sī sus (dē + *rīdeō), laugh at, have the laugh on (someone)
dēscendō ere dī sus, come down
dēsistō ere stitī stitus, desist from, stop (+ infinitive)
dētrahō ere trāxī trāctus (dē + trahō), pull off, take off
deus ī m, god
dēvorō āre āvī ātus, devour, swallow
dexter tra trum, right
dīcō ere dīxī dictus, say, tell, mention, speak; *male dicere* (+ dat.), revile
dictum ī n, word, quïp, pun, lofty sentiment
dīdūcō ere dūxī ductus, draw apart, open up
diēs ēī m, day
difficilis e, difficult
*digitus ī m, finger
dīgnus a um, deserving, worthy
dīligenter, carefully, scrupulously
*discō ere didicī, learn
discordia ae f, discord, mere noise
*discumbō ere cubuī cubitus, lean, lie, recline (at table)
discurrō ere currī cursus, run about, scatter
diū, long, for a long time; *diūtius*, longer, for quite a long time
dīvidō ere vīsī vīsus, divide, distribute
dīvīnus a um, divine
dō dare dedī datus, give, utter
doceō ēre uī ctus, teach
*domina ae f, mistress
*dominus ī m, master
domus ūs f, house, home; *domī*, at home, on the place (estate)
dubitō āre āvī ātus, hesitate
ducentī ae a, two hundred
dūcō ere dūxī ductus, lead, take, escort, attract
*dūdum: See *jam*.

dum, while, when, in the act of
duo duae duo, two
duodecim, twelve

ē, ex, out of, from, of
*ēbrietās tātis f, intoxication
*ēbrius a um, drunk, drunken
*ecce, lo and behold, look, see, see here now
ēdūcō ere dūxī ductus, take aside
efficiō ere fēcī fectus (ex + faciō), cause, bring about
effluō ere fluxī (ex + fluō), flow out, spill
effringō ere frēgī frāctus (ex + frangō), break down
effugiō ere fūgī (ex + fugiō), escape
*effundō ere fūdī fūsus (ex + *fundō), pour out
effūsē, effusively; cp. *effundō.
ego meī, I
*ēheu or heu, alas, alack, welladay, dear me
*ejusmodī (= ejus modī), of this sort, that kind of
ēlegāns antis, elegant
ēloquentia ae f, eloquence
ēmittō ere mīsī missus, let out
emō ere ēmī emptus, buy
enim, for, no doubt, indeed, in fact
eō īre īvī or iī itum, go
epigramma atis n, epigram
equus ī m, horse
ērēctus a um, erect, upright
*ergō, therefore, so; then, well!
*errō āre āvī ātus, wander about, be mistaken
estō, be (fut. imperat. of *sum)*
et, and, also, too, even; *et . . . et*, both . . . and
etiam, also, even
etsī, even if, although
ēvertō ere tī sus (ē + vertō), turn upside down, upset
ēvītō āre āvī ātus (ē + vītō), avoid

*ēvolō āre āvī ātus (ē + *volō, fly), fly out
excipiō ere cēpī ceptus (ex + capiō), take up, catch, react to
exclāmō āre āvī ātus, exclaim, shout, shout out, shriek
exeāmus: Review eō, īre.
exeō īre īvī or iī itum, go out, go off, come out
exerceō ēre uī itus, exercise
exhortor ārī ātus sum, encourage
exitus ūs m, departure, death, end
exōrō āre āvī ātus, beg or beseech (a person, acc.) for (something, acc.)
expectātiō ōnis f, expectation
expectō āre āvī ātus, expect, await, watch to see
experior īrī pertus sum, test, find out
expīrō āre āvī ātus, expire, die
expōnō ere posuī positus, set forth, explain
*exsurgō ere surrēxī (ex + *surgō), rise up, get up (from table)
extendō ere dī tus or sus, extend, stretch, pit
extrā, outside of, out of
extrahō ere trāxī tractus, pull out
extremus a um, last

*fābula ae f, talk, story
faciēs ēī f, face
facilis e, easy
faciō ere fēcī factus, do, make, build, represent, grant, value, regard as worth (+ gen.)
factum ī n, deed, a happening
famēs is f, hunger
familia ae f, family, household, slaves; see on tota familia, 31b.
famōsus a um, famous, notorious
fātum ī n, fate, luck
*fēlīcitās tātis f, happiness, prosperity
*fēlīciter, fortunately, luckily; see note on 50a.

fēlīx īcis, fortunate, happy, prosperous
*ferculum ī n, dish, course (of a dinner)
ferō ferre tulī lātus, carry, bear, bring
ferrum ī n, iron, steel, sword, finger ring (made of iron)
fidēlis e, faithful, reliable
fidēs eī f, reputation, faith, credit (in business)
fīgō ere fīxī fīxus, fasten, fasten down or up, post
figūra ae f, figure, shape, form
fīlia ae f, daughter
fīlius ī m, son
fīniō īre īvī ītus, finish
fīnis is m, end; plural, territories
fīō fierī factus sum, be done, be made, become, take place, turn into, happen
fleō ēre flēvī flētus, cry, weep
fluō ere fluxī fluctus, flow
forma ae f, form, proportions, good looks, beauty
forte, by chance; forte vēnit, he happened to come
fortis e, brave, courageous, steady
fortitūdō dinis f, bravery, courage, strength
fortūna ae f, fortune, Fortune, luck
forum ī n, forum, downtown business section
frangō ere frēgī frāctus, break
frāter tris m, brother
frequenter, frequently
frōns frontis f, brow, forehead, front
fuga ae f, flight, escape
fugiō ere fūgī, flee, escape
furor ōris m, fury

Gāius Gāī, Gaius, master, boss; see on Fortūnāta, 37a, and fēlīciter, 50a.

*genius ī m, genius; see note on 37a.
genus eris n, kind, sort, family line
geōmetria ae f, geometry
gesticulor ārī ātus sum, gesticulate, use pantomime gestures
gladius ī m, sword
glōriōsus a um, glorious, chic, swanky
Graecus a um, Greek
grandis e, grand, great
grātia ae f, gratitude, thanks; grātiās agere, to thank
gravis e, heavy
graviter, heavily
*gustō āre āvī ātus, taste, eat

habeō ēre uī itus, have, consider
habitō āre āvī ātus, dwell, live
hasta ae f, spear
*heu or ēheu, alas, alack, welladay, dear me
hīc, here, now, at this point
hic haec hoc, this, these, this man, this thing; he, she, it, etc.
*hilarē, gaily, merrily
*hilaris e, gay, merry
*hilaritās tātis f, gaiety, merriment, fun
*hinc, from this point, then, next
*hodiē, today
homō inis m, f, man, creature, gent, fellow
*honestē, respectably
*honestus a um, respectable
honōrātus a um, honored
hōra ae f, hour, time of day
horribilis e, horrible, dreadful
hortor ārī ātus sum, urge, exhort
hūmānus a um, human

ibi, there, at that point
īdem eadem idem, same, the same
*ideō, for that reason, that's the reason why
idōneus a um, suitable

igitur, then, accordingly
*īgnōscō ere nōvī nōtus, excuse
ille illa illud, that, those, that man, that thing; he, she, it, etc.
*imitor ārī ātus sum, imitate
immittō ere mīsī missus (in + mittō), let go in, put on.
thrust, fling
*immō, rather, on the contrary, in fact, furthermore
imperō āre āvī ātus, command
impleō ēre ēvī ētus (in + pleō), fill, fill up
impōnō ere posuī positus (in + pōnō), put on, place on, give in, in, on, at; into, onto, to, till, into the midst of
incendium ī n, a fire
incendō ere dī sus, burn
incipiō ere cēpī ceptus (in + capiō), begin
*incumbō ere cubuī cubitus (Cp. *discumbō), lean
inde, then, next, out of it
indecenter, indecently, shamelessly, impolitely
India ae f, India
indicō āre āvī ātus, indicate, explain
indīgnātus a um, indignant
indīgnus a um, unworthy, outrageous
indulgentia ae f, indulgence, kindness
*īnfēlīx īcis (Cp. fēlīx), unfortunate
īnferior ius, lower
īnflātus a um, inflated
*īnfundō ere fūdī fusus (Cp. *effundō), pour into, pour over
ingeniōsus a um, ingenious, smart, clever
*ingēns entis, huge, great
ingrātus a um, unpleasant, thankless
inimīcus a um, unfriendly, enemy
initium ī n, a beginning
injūria ae f, injury
inquam inquis inquit inquiunt, say

125

īnscrībō ere psī ptus, inscribe
īnscrīptiō ōnis f, inscription,
    epitaph
īnsequor ī secūtus sum, follow,
    come after, come next
īnspiciō ere spēxī spectus,
    examine, look to see
intellegō ere lēxī lēctus, realize,
    understand
inter, among, between, with, at,
    in the midst of
intereā, meanwhile
intereō īre īvī iī itum, die out
interim, meanwhile
intermittō ere mīsī missus,
    interrupt
interpōnō ere posuī positus,
    interpose, allow to elapse
interpres etis m, f, interpreter
interrogō āre āvī ātus, ask
interventus ūs m, intervention
intestīnum ī n (f. in vulgar Latin),
    a gut; plural, intestines,
    insides
intrā, inside, among
*intrō āre āvī ātus, enter
inveniō īre vēnī ventus (in +
    veniō), come upon, find
invītō āre āvī ātus, invite
*involvō ere vī ūtus (in +
    *volvō), roll, roll up, wrap up,
    bandage
ipse ipsa ipsum, self, myself,
    yourself, himself, etc.; the
    very (one), etc.
*īrāscor ī īrātus sum, be angry
    (+ dative)
is ea id, the, this, these, that,
    those, the one; he, she, it, etc.
iste ista istud, that, those; he,
    she, it, etc.
ita, so, in such a way; well!
itaque, and so
iter itineris n, way

*jaceō ēre uī, lie (prostrate)
jaciō ere jēcī jactus, throw
jam, now, already, by this time,
    soon; *jam dūdum, long before
    this

*jānua ae f, door
jubeō ēre jussī jussus, order,
    tell
Juppiter Jovis m, Jupiter
jūrō āre āvī ātus, swear
jūs jūris n, right, law, duty
juvō āre jūvī jūtus, help, delight,
    please

labōriōsus a um, laborious,
    hardworking, busy
labōrō āre āvī ātus, be in dis-
    tress, feel (the) strain
*labrum ī n, lip
*lacerō āre āvī ātus, lacerate,
    cut to pieces, butcher, carve
lāmentātiō ōnis f, lamentation
*lāna ae f, wool
latus eris n, side
laudātiō ōnis f, praise, applause
laudō āre āvī ātus, praise, com-
    mend
*lautitia ae f, elegance, luxury
*lautus a um, elegant, swell;
    lit. washed − cp. *lavō.
*lavō āre lāvī lautus, wash,
    bathe, launder; passive, take
    a bath
*lectus ī m, bed, couch
*legō ere lēgī lēctus, read
levis e, light, fickle
*libenter, gladly
liber brī m, book
līber era erum, free
lībertās tātis f, liberty, freedom
*lībertus ī m, freedman; see
    Introduction, page 37.
licet ēre uit or licitum est, it is
    permitted, one may
*lingua ae f, tongue, language,
    lingo
littera ae f, letter (of alphabet);
    plural, literature, learning −
    see note on *satis inquinatus*,
    46c.
līvidus a um, livid, black and
    blue
locus ī m, place, spot, point
longē, far
longus a um, long, tall

126

loquor ī locutūs sum, talk, speak, say

lūceō ēre lūxī (Cp. *lūx*), be light, shine

*lucerna ae f, lamp

lūna ae f, moon

lūx lūcis f, light, daylight

magis, more, the more, rather

māgnitūdō dinis f, magnitude

māgnus a um, big, great, loud, tall

mājor mājus, bigger, larger

male, badly

māllem: Review *mālō*.

mālō mālle māluī, prefer, like better

malus a um, bad, poor, evil, wicked

*manū mittō, manumit; see note on *manū mīsit*, 42c.

manus ūs f, hand

margō inis m, margin, edge

māssa ae f, mass

māter tris f, mother

māvult: Review *mālō*.

māximus a um, greatest, very great

*medicus ī m, doctor

medius a um, (the) middle (of); *in mediō*, inside, right there, in here; *in medium*, into the middle of the room, etc.; *dē mediō*, away with . . .

*meherculēs, by Hercules, by - - -

melior melius, better

*meminī isse (+ gen.), remember

memoria ae f, memory

mēns mentis f, mind, attitude

*mēnsa ae f, table

mēnsis is m, month

mentiō ōnis f, mention

*mentior īrī mentītus sum, lie, tell a lie

merīdiēs (eī) m, noon

meus a um, my, my own

mīles itis m, soldier

mīlle, a thousand

minimē, by no means

minimus a um, smallest, slightest, tiny

minor minus, smaller, less

minus, less; *nōn minus*, no less, likewise; *nihilō minus*, none the less; *plūs minus*, more or less; *nec minus*, and also

minūtus a um, minute, miniature, tiny

mīror ārī ātus sum, admire, express astonishment at, be astonished, wonder

*misellus a um (Cp. *miser*), poor old, poor little

miser era erum, wretched, pitiful

mittō ere mīsī missus, let go, send, direct

mōbilis e, moveable, flexible

modo, not so long ago, just, just a little while ago; *modo* . . . *modo*, at one time . . . at another time

modus ī m, measure, amount, way, kind

*molestus a um, vexatious, boresome

mōmentum ī n, moment

mōnstrōsus a um, monstrous, revolting

*monumentum ī n, monument, tomb

mora ae f, delay

*morior ī mortuus moritūrus, die

moror ārī ātus sum, delay, bore

mors mortis f, death

mōs mōris m, custom, fashion

moveō ēre mōvī motus, move, arouse, annoy

mox, soon

mulier eris f, woman

multō, (by) much

multus a um, many, much

mūnus eris n, service, duty, gift

*mūs mūris m, f, mouse

mūtō āre āvī ātus, change

mūtus a um, mute, dumb

nam, for, indeed

nancīscor ī nactus or nanctus sum, get, gain, obtain

nārrō āre āvī ātus, tell
nāscor ī nātus sum, be born, be
  produced
nātūra ae f, nature
nausea ae f, nausea, sickness at
  the stomach, disgust, loath-
  someness
nāvigō āre āvī ātus, sail
nāvis is f, ship
nē, lest, that . . . not; (fearing)
  that; nē . . . quidem, not even
nec (= neque), and not, nor;
  nec . . . nec, neither . . . nor
necesse habēre, to find it necessary
negligentia ae f, negligence
negō āre āvī ātus, deny, say no
negōtium ī n, business, job
nēmō nēminī nēminem, no one,
  none
neque (= nec), and not, nor;
  neque . . . neque, neither . . .
  nor
*nesciō īre īvī, not know
neuter tra trum, neither
*niger gra grum, black
nihil nihilō, nothing; nihilō
  minus, nevertheless, none
  the less; as adverb, not at all
nīl (= nihil), nothing
nisi, if . . . not, unless, had it
  not been that . . .; except
nōlō nōlle nōluī, be unwilling,
  not want, refuse; nōlī or
  nōlīte + infinitive, don't
nōmen inis n, name
nōn, not
nōndum, not yet
nōs nostrum, we
nōscō ere nōvī nōtus, learn, become acquainted with; perfect,
  know
noster tra trum, our
nōstī: Review nōscō.
*notō āre āvī ātus, notice, ob-
  serve
nōvī: Review nōscō.
novus a um, new, unusual
nox noctis f, night
nūdus a um, nude, bare, naked

nūllus a um, not any, not one,
  no, no one
numerō āre āvī ātus, count
numerus ī m, number; ad
  numerum, equally
numquam, never
nunc, now, as things are
nūntiō āre āvī ātus, announce

ob, on account of, because of
obligātus a um, obligated, ob-
  liged
*oblīvīscor ī oblītus sum (+
  genit.) forget
occāsiō ōnis f, opportunity
occīdō ere cīdī cīsus, kill
occupō āre āvī ātus, take possession of
occurrō ere currī cursus (ob +
  currō), run up (to)
oculus ī m, eye; ab oculō, at
  sight
offendō ere fendī fēnsus, offend
officiōsus a um, officious
officium ī n, duty, function
olīva ae f, olive
Olympius a um, Olympian
omnis e, all, every
*onerō āre āvī ātus, load
onus eris n, load, burden, a
  heavy pack
opera ae f, exertion, work;
  operam dare, take pains,
  exert oneself
oportet ēre uit, it is right, one
  ought, it must be (that) . . .
opportūnus a um, opportune,
  convenient, welcome
opprimō ere pressī pressus (ob +
  premō) oppress, exploit
(ops) opis f, help
optimē, very well, impressively
optimus a um, best
ōrātor ōris m, orator
*Orcus ī m, Orcus, god of the
  Lower World; hell, death
ōrō āre āvī ātus, beg, pray
*ōs ōris n, mouth
*ōsculor ārī ātus sum, kiss
ostendō ere dī tus, display, show

paene, almost
*pānis is m, bread, loaf, piece
  of bread
pār paris, equal, proper, right
*parātus a um, ready, prompt
parcō ere pepercī parsus, spare,
  be easy on
parō āre āvī ātus, prepare, ac-
  quire
pars partis f, part, side, direc-
  tion
parvus a um, little
pater tris m, father
patior ī passus sum, allow
patria ae f, one's country, country
*patrimōnium ī n, patrimony,
  estate
patrōnus ī m, patron; see Introduction, page 37.
paucus a um, few
paulisper, for a moment, for a
  short time
paulō, (by) a little
*pauper peris, poor, a poor man
pecūnia ae f, money
pecus oris n, herd, flock, sheep
pējor pējus, worse
pendeō ēre pependī, be sus-
  pended, hang
per, through, by, along, down
*perbāsiō āre āvī ātus, kiss
  thoroughly
*percutiō ere cussī cussus,
  strike, knock at
perdō ere perdidi perditus, lose,
  ruin
perdūcō ere dūxī ductus, bring
pereō īre īvī iī itum, pass away,
  perish
*perfundō ere fūdī fūsus (Cp.
  *īnfundo), pour over, drench
perīculum ī n, danger, risk
permittō ere mīsī missus, permit
persequor ī secūtus sum, follow
  up, chase
persuādeō ēre sī sus, persuade
pertineō ēre uī, pertain
perveniō īre vēnī ventus (+ ad),
  arrive at, reach

pēs pedis m, foot
pessimē, in the worst way
petō ere īvī ītus, seek, make for,
  go to, request something of
  (ab) a person
philosophus ī m, philosopher
pictūra ae f, picture, painting
*pingō ere pinxī pictus, paint,
  depict
*piscis is m, fish
placeō ēre uī itus, please, be
  pleasing, find favor, be de-
  cided upon
*plānē, clearly, obviously,
  utterly
*plaudō ere sī sus, clap the
  hands, applaud
*plausus ūs m, applause
*plēnus a um, full, bountiful,
  full spread
*plōrō āre āvī ātus, mourn, weep
  for, weep
plūs plūris, more; plūs minus,
  more or less
poēma atis n, poem
poena ae f, punishment
poēta ae m, poet
pōnō ere posuī positus, put,
  place, set; serve (food)
populus ī m, people
*porcus ī m, pig
portō āre āvī atus, carry
pōscō ere popōscī, ask for,
  demand
*possideō ēre sēdī sessus, pos-
  sess
possum posse potui, be able,
  can, could
post, after, behind
posteā, later, after this, here-
  after
postquam, after, when
potestās tātis f, opportunity
*pōtiō ōnis f, a drink
prae, in front of, because of
praecēdō ere cessī cessus, lead
  the way
praecipuē, especially
praepōnō ere posuī positus, put
  before, put in charge of

129

praesēns entis, present
praesidium ī n, garrison, guard
praestō āre stitī stitus, set or
    stand before
praeter, except
praintereā, besides
prex precis f, prayer, plea
prīdiē, the day before
prīmitus, at first
prīmum, first, for the first time
prīmus a um, first
prīvātus a um, private
prō, on behalf of, instead of, for,
    in accordance with
probō āre āvī ātus, prove, test
prōcēdō ere cessī cessus, pro-
    ceed, come forward
prōclāmō āre āvī ātus, proclaim,
    shout out, scream
prōcurrō ere cucurrī cursus, run
    forward
prōdeō īre īvī or iī itus, go
    forward
prōferō ferre tulī lātus, bring
    out, bring forth, take out
prōjiciō ere jēcī jectus (prō +
    jaciō), throw, throw out,
    throw down
properō āre āvī ātus, hurry
propter, on account of
prōscrībō ere psī ptus, advertise
prōsequor ī secūtus sum, follow
    up
prōtulit: Review *ferō.*
prōvideō ēre vīdī vīsus, look
    ahead
prōvocō āre āvī ātus, challenge
proximē, recently
proximus a um, next, next to
prūdēns entis, prudent, sophis-
    ticated, wise
pūblicus a um, public, open,
    outside
puer erī m, boy, slave boy
pūgna ae f, fight
pulcher chra chrum, handsome,
    pretty
pūrus a um, pure
putō āre āvī ātus, think, con-
    sider, imagine, suppose

quadrāgēsimus a um, fortieth
quadrāgintā, forty
quaerō ere sīvī sītus, look for,
    ask, devise
quam, than, rather than; how!
    tam . . . quam, so much . . . as
quamdiū, as long as
quantus a um, how great, how
    much; *quantī,* at what price
*quārē (quā + rē), so, therefore;
    why
quattuor, four
−que, and
*quemadmodum, how, as
queror ī questus sum, complain
    (of)
quī quae quod (relative), who,
    whose, whom; the man who,
    the thing which; that, that
    which, which; whoever, what-
    ever; he, she, it, etc.
*quia, because
quid, why? what for?
quīdam quaedam quoddam, some,
    someone, something; a certain
    person, etc.
quidem, indeed, of course, of all
    things! *nē . . . quidem,* not
    even
quiēs ētis f, rest
quīnque, five
quīntus a um, fifth
quis or quī, quae or qua, quid or
    quod (indefinite), some, any;
    anyone, anything
quis or quī, quae, quid or quod
    (interrogative), who? whose?
    whom? what? which?
quisquam quicquam, anyone,
    anything
quisque quaeque quidque, each,
    each one, everyone
*quisquis quicquid, whoever,
    whatever
quō, where
quod, because, as; that which, a
    thing which; the fact that, as
    for the fact that; cp. *quod sī.*
*quod sī, but if, and if

*quōmodo, how, as
quoque, also

rapiō ere uī ptus, seize, whisk
away
ratiō ōnis f, account, reasoning,
way, device, scheme
recipiō ere cēpī ceptus (re +
capiō), receive, get back
recitō āre āvī ātus, recite, read
aloud
recreātus a um, re-created, re-
stored, reassured
recūsō āre āvī ātus, refuse
reddō ere redidī reditus, give
back, pay back; depict
redeō īre īvī iī itum, go back,
come back, return
redimō ere ēmī ēmptus (red +
emō), buy, buy back, ransom
referō ferre rettulī relātus, bring,
bring back, draw back, return
reficiō ere fēcī fectus (re +
faciō), make over, repair,
renew, revive
relaxātus a um, relaxed
relēgō āre āvī ātus, relegate
religiōsus a um, religious
relinquō ere līquī lictus, leave,
leave behind, bequeath
reliquiae ārum f, leftovers
reliquus a um, the other, the
rest of
remittō ere mīsī missus, remit,
send back, revoke
*reor rērī ratus sum, think,
suppose
repentē, suddenly
repetō ere petīvī petītus, seek
again, take up again
repleō ēre ēvī ētus, fill, fill up
repōnō ere posuī positus, put
back, replace
*repositōrium ī n, tray
res reī f, thing, matter, stuff,
affair
resolvō ere solvī solūtus, un-
fasten
respiciō ere spēxī spectus,
look, look at, look back

respondeō ēre dī sus, answer,
reply
rettulī: Review referō.
revertor ī sus sum, return, come
back, go back
rēx rēgis m, king
*rīdeō ēre rīsī rīsus, laugh,
laugh at
*rīsus ūs m, laughter
rogō āre āvī ātus, ask, beg, beg
for, plead, invite; parenthetical
rogo, please!
Rōma ae f, Rome
Rōmānus a um, Roman
rūrsus, again, in turn

sacer cra crum, sacred
saepe, often; saepius, oftener,
quite often
*salvus a um, safe, unharmed,
alive
*sānē, really, indeed
satis, enough, sufficiently,
rather well, quite; satis faciō,
give satisfaction
*scīlicet (scīre + licet), of
course, naturally
sciō scīre īvī ītus, know
scrībō ere psī ptus, write
scūtum ī n, shield
sēcrētō, secretly
*secundum (+ acc.), next to,
beside
secundus a um, second
sed, but
*sedeō ēre sēdī sessus, sit, sit
down
*semel, once
sēmihōra ae f, half an hour
semper, always, all the time, for
ever
sempiternō, for ever
sentiō īre sēnsī sēnsus, feel
sepulcrum ī n, sepulcher, grave
sequor ī secūtus sum, follow
*sermō ōnis m, conversation, talk
servitūs ūtis f, servitude,
slavery
servō āre āvī ātus, protect, save,
keep, observe

131

servulus ī m, little slave
servus ī m, slave
sī, if, whether
sīc, so, thus; sīc . . . ut, in such
a way that; sīc . . . tamquam,
just like
sīcut, as, just as, like
sīgnum ī n, signal
silentium ī n, silence
silva ae f, a wood
silvāticus a um, woodsy
sine, without
singulī ae a, one by one
sinister tra trum, left
*sinus ūs m, a curve, fold, or
hollow; the curved fold of the
toga across the breast, which
was used as a pocket; hence,
pocket, breast, bosom, or lap
sīve, or if; sīve . . . sīve,
whether . . . or
socius ī m, companion
*soleō ēre − solitus, be ac-
customed
sōlus a um, only, alone
solvō ere solvī solūtus, release,
pay
*sonō āre uī itus, make a sound
or a noise
*sonus ī m, sound, noise
sordidus a um, sordid, dirty
soror ōris f, sister
*spargō ere sī sus, sprinkle,
scatter, spatter
spatium ī n, space, interval
spectāculum ī n, spectacle,
scene
spectō āre āvī ātus, look, watch
spērō āre āvī ātus, hope
statim, at once, immediately
statua ae f, statue
stō stāre stetī status, stand
*stringō ere nxī ctus, draw, un-
sheathe
studium ī n, zeal, eagerness,
devotion; plural, studies
*suādeō ēre sī sus, persuade,
urge, advise
*suāvis e, pleasant; suāviter,
pleasantly; solēbās suāvius

esse, you used to be more
fun − see on suāvius, 33a,
and cp. bene in vocab.
sub, under
subeō īre īvī iī itus, go under,
enter, succeed, replace
*subinde, repeatedly
subitō, suddenly
sublātus: Review tollō.
subsequor ī secūtus sum,
follow close behind
suī sibi sē sē, him(self),
her(self), it(self),
them(selves); each other
sum esse fuī futūrus, be
*summa ae f, top, summit, total,
essence; ad summam, in short,
'smatter of fact
summus a um, topmost, the top
of, the height of
sūmō ere sūmpsī sūmptus, take
*super (+ acc.), above, over, on
top of, next (at table)
superior ius, upper
suppōnō ere posuī positus (sub
+ pōnō), put in place of
supprimō ere pressī pressus
(sub + premō), suppress,
restrain
suprā, above, next (at table)
*surgō ere surrēxī (cp. *cōn-
surgō), rise up, get up
suspīciō ōnis f, suspicion
suspicor ārī ātus sum, suspect
sustineō ēre tinuī tentus (subs
+ teneō), hold up
sustulī: Review tollō.
suus a um, his (own), her (own),
its (own), their (own)
*symphōnia ae f, orchestra; see
ad.

*taceō ēre tacuī tacitus, be
silent
tam, so, such; tam . . . quam,
as . . . as, so much . . . as,
just the same . . . as
tamen, however, nevertheless

*tamquam, as much as, as, as if, just like; *sīc . . . tamquam,* just like

tandem, at last

tangō ere tetigī tāctus, touch

tantus a um, so great, so large; *tantō,* (by) so much; *tantī,* of such value

tēctum ī n, roof

tegō ere tēxī tēctus, cover, protect

tempestās tātis f, weather

templum ī n, temple

temptō āre āvī ātus, attempt, try, test

tempus oris n, time

teneō ēre uī, hold, hold back, keep, grasp, occupy, contain

*tergeō ēre sī sus, wipe

terra ae f, earth, ground, floor

tertius a um, third

tetigī: Review *tangō.*

timeō ēre uī, fear

timidus a um, timid, shaking, fearful

timor ōris m, fear

tolerābilis e, tolerable, endurable

tollō ere sustulī sublātus, lift up, pick up, raise, take, take away, withdraw

*torus ī m, couch, dining couch

tot, so many

tōtus a um, whole, the whole (of), all, entire

trahō ere trāxī tractus, draw, drag

trājiciō ere jēcī jectus (trāns + jaciō), throw across, transfer, transfix, pierce

trānseō īre īvī or iī itum, go across, cross, pass by

trecentī ae a, three hundred

trepidātiō ōnis f, trepidation, fear

trēs tria, three

*trīclīnium ī n, dining room

trīduum ī n, a period of three days

trīgintā, thirty

tū tuī, you, yourself (singular)

tuba ae f, tuba, trumpet

tueor ērī tūtus sum, watch, protect, maintain

tum, then

tumultus ūs m, tumult, commotion, uproar

*tunc, then, at that time

*tunica ae f, tunic

turpis e, shameful

tuus a um, your, your own

ubi, where, when, in which, on which, in matters in which

ūllus a um, any

ūltimus a um, last; *ūltimō,* ultimately, finally, at last

ūltrō, of one's own free will

umquam, ever

unde, (from) where, from which, with which

*unguentum ī n, perfume

ūniversus a um, all, all together

ūnus a um, a, one

urna ae f, urn

ūsque, all the way, even to

ut, that, so that, as, when

*utique, anyhow, especially

ūtor ī ūsus sum, use, enjoy, indulge in

utrum . . . an, whether . . . or

uxor ōris f, wife

*valdē, very, very much

valeō ēre uī itūrus, be strong, be worth

varius a um, various

vehementer, violently, strongly, greatly

vehō ere vexī vectus, carry, convey

vel, or; even

velle: Review *volō.*

*vēndō ere didī, sell

veniō īre vēnī ventum, come

verbum ī n, word

vereor ērī veritus sum, fear, be afraid

vērō, really, in fact, but

versus ūs m, verse

133

vērus a um, true, real
vester tra trum, your, your own
*vestīmentum ī n, garment;
   plural, clothes
vestis is f, garment, clothing
via ae f, way, path, road, street
videō ēre vīdī vīsus, see, notice,
   consider; passive, seem, look
   like, seem good, be agreeable
vigilō āre āvī ātus, stand guard,
   be awake
vīgintī, twenty
vīlla ae f, villa, country place,
   farm
vincō ere vīcī vīctus, conquer
*vīnum ī n, wine
vir virī m, man
virtūs tūtis f, manliness, ex-
cellence, worth, pluck
vīta ae f, life
*vitreus a um, (made of) glass
vīvō ere vīxī, live, be alive,
   last
vīvus a um, alive, living
vix, scarcely, hardly
vocō āre āvī ātus, call
*volō āre āvī, fly
volō velle voluī, wish, want, be
   willing
vōs vestrum, you, yourselves
vōx vōcis f, voice, word, sound
vulnerō āre āvī ātus, wound
vulnus eris n, wound, slit
vultis: Review *volō*.
*vultus ūs m, face, countenance,
   glance

Jacob E. Nyenhuis is Associate Professor and chairman of the department of Greek and Latin, and director of the Liberal Arts Honors Program, Wayne State University.

The manuscript was prepared for publication by Sandra Shapiro. This book was designed by Mary Jowski. The typeface used is Baskerville, designed by John Baskerville in the eighteenth century. The display face used is Perpetua, designed by Eric Gill in 1920. The paper used is Warren's Olde Style Antique. Manufactured in the United States of America.